·THE·
Archive Photographs
SERIES

SOUTH THAMES
TOWER BRIDGE TO THAMESMEAD

Thames sailing barge. PLA

THE
Archive Photographs
SERIES

SOUTH THAMES
TOWER BRIDGE TO THAMESMEAD

Compiled by
Hilary Heffernan

CHALFORD

First published 1996
Copyright © Hilary Heffernan, 1996

The Chalford Publishing Company
St Mary's Mill, Chalford,
Stroud, Gloucestershire, GL6 8NX

ISBN 0 7524 0670 1

Typesetting and origination by
The Chalford Publishing Company
Printed in Great Britain by
Redwood Books, Trowbridge

Aerial view of the Thames from Tower Bridge to Thamesmead, showing the five great upriver dock systems of the Port of London Authority in 1961. PLA

Contents

Acknowledgements

This book is dedicated to my father, Walter 'Jake' Steeple, a historian whose enduring affinity with the Thames, the sea and all things nautical was passed on to his family: he would have loved to have helped with my research. As a Leading Seaman aboard HMS *Roi Leopold*, Jake was one of the many who sailed to Normany on D-Day to help rescue British soldiers stranded on the beaches.

My sincere thanks and appreciation are expressed to:

Bob Aspinall, PLA Museum in Docklands • Sir John Bartlett • Gus Baulch, London Dockworker • PC John Bonnewell • John Brownfield, rtd Deputy Headmaster • Joyce Bullemore • Ted Callan, Waterman • Glenn Carroll, Holiday Inn, Nelson Dk • C.F. Cato Carter • Len Coker, Waterman • Commander Mike 'John' Cooley and the Captain and Officers of HMS Gloucester • Robert George Crouch, Bargemaster to H.M. the Queen • Mrs June Darby • Ben Dillon, Waterman • Sidney Fagan, MA • Mrs Nell Griffin • PC Keith Gotch, Thames Division, Wapping • Adam Harper, Design Engineeer • Captain Maurice Jones • John Hibbert, shipping agent • Donald Hunt, Lay Admin. St Mary Magdalene, Woolwich • Ronald Hunt, retired director and general wharf manager, Cawoods • Barbara Lewis, HM Customs and Excise • Mary Lowrie, Tower Bridge Experience • Maurice Lyne, Royal Waterman • Percivals Camera Centre, Eltham • D.W. Richards • Mrs Dolly Sargent • Peter Sargent, Waterman and Transporting River Pilot • Bill Shrieve • Harry Skelton, Waterman and Ivy Skelton MBE • Julian Watson, Greenwich Local History Library, Blackheath • Enid Webb, St Mary Magdalene, Woolwich and Tony and Yvonne Wheatley, who have all given invaluable support, supplied information, documents, photographs, research and sailing opportunites and proof-read scripts to check the accuracy of my facts.

My gratitude for the use of copyright material goes to the Police Association, Wapping, Metropolitan Police Thames Division Museum (pictures identified: MPTD), HM Customs and Excise, Liverpool (pictures identified: HMC&E), Port of London Authority Museum in Docklands (pictures identified: PLA), Greenwich Local History Library, Blackheath (pictures identified: GLHL). Finally, my thanks and apologies go to anyone whose material or help has contributed to this book's production but whom I have inadvertently failed to acknowledge by name.

Introduction

'I was born at Greenwich in 1916' recalls retired lighterman Len Coker 'and from the age of ten hung around the pier alongside Garden Steps and Ship Hotel before the *Cutty Sark* was there. For a shilling a time us kids used to help the old boatmen: there were five of them whose living it was to row the seaman off to their sugar ships moored off Greenwich Buoys. These boatmen liked to take a drink, so when trade was slack they left us to row about in their boats while they went off for a few pints. 'One day I'd been holding off a boat for about 1½ hours for a boatman who was in The Ship when he came to The Steps shouting for me to come in. He was dressed in a peaked cap, long overcoat and smoking a "cig". I could see he was the worse for drink so thought I'd turn the boat around and back it in stern first as the stern was lower in the water and easier for him to climb aboard. Anyway, I was still backing when he thought the boat was already in. He stepped out into the water, missed the boat completely and sank. I got his hand onto the side of the boat and at the same time he felt his feet touch the bottom: he was standing on The Steps. He walked up five steps, sat down all dripping wet and tried to light the cig' he still had in his mouth from when he went in. He gave me 2d and I ran home, scared out of life' laughed Len.

The Thames, at once a physical and social barrier, water-highway and gateway to empires, is one of the world's most fascinating rivers. Anyone working or living near it or who dealt with it in any one way has tales to tell which keep memories alive and return them and us to its swirling, living waters time and again. From early time most of the working side of the river was on the south. Invading Romans crossed from south to north in the vicinity of the present London Bridge. Traders sailed upriver from over the Channel, bartering their goods on both shores. Many famous ships are associated with South Thames. Henry VIII's *Great Harry* and Sir Francis Drake's *Golden Hind* were launched from Deptford and Woolwich. The Pilgrim Fathers' *Mayflower* was built at Rotherhithe: a pub, formerly The Spread Eagle and Cushion, now marks the site. *Temeraire*, 98 guns and 750 crew, broken up in John Beatson's Rotherhithe shipyard, 1838, cost £60,000 and 5,000 royal oak trees to build and fought alongside *Victory* at Trafalgar. Her salvage value was £5,500; Turner's painting 'The Fighting Temeraire', is in Greenwich National Maritime Museum. The clipper ship, *Cutty Sark*, and Sir Francis Chichester's *Gipsy Moth* are both drydocked in Greenwich.

Royalty have long been regular users of London's watery highway, ferried in opulent, carved and gilded scarlet and gold barges powered by Royal Watermen. These Royal barges can still be seen at the National Maritime Museum. The sleek *Royal Nore* continues this tradition. In celebration of the succession of George I to the throne, Handel wrote his *Water Music*. Frances Drake received his knighthood on the Deptford quayside from H.M. Queen Elizabeth I: Frances Chichester, round-the-world yachtsman, was knighted in Grand Square, Greenwich Royal Navy College four centuries later by H.M. Queen Elizabeth II using the same sword. Peter the Great, Czar of Russia, laboured in Deptford dockyards, learning first hand the boatbuilders craft. These were proud times. By the seventeenth century London was the cultural and social centre of the known world. Trade was brisk. Fortunes were made and lost by merchants and the wealthy speculating on cargoes carried across hazardous seas in often overloaded ships, some little bigger than a decent-sized modern yacht. At this time south of the river was very different.

To the north was The City's square mile of affluent business houses, royal palaces, home of the money-fabricating Mint, Bank of England, wealthy Guilds and a glittering show case for the opulent. Beyond the social pale yet linked over time by bridge, foot tunnels, ferries and wherries was South London; bustling home to workmen, vagabonds, tenements, hospices for the poor, thieves, lively theatres and itinerant actors, annual jollities such as Horne and Southwark Fairs, inns and bawdy houses. It was the working side of London where ships were built, repaired and victualled, labourers lived in overcrowded slums while footpads and highwaymen laid wait for the unwary on their way by coach to Dover and France.

There are distinctions between the different kinds of river workers: Stevedores (frequently overseers) and dockers loaded ships. Lightermen, working thirty-foot sweeps or oars with dexterity, moved often cumbersome loads, lightening ships, dealing with barges and tugs. Watermen, formerly taxidrivers of the Thames, plied their trade from Steps till leading down to the river. Thomas Doggett, Dublin comedian, came to London in 1691, frequently using the services of Thames watermen, was so impressed by their skills he instituted an annual race for newly appointed Freemen for the river. The prize was a splendid badge and scarlet coat for which Thames watermen still scull. Doggett, buried at Eltham, died a pauper. By paying a few pence for the crossing a wealthy lord could sample unsavoury delights at the bearpits, cockfights or gambling dens while risking losing his purse or his life among seedy back streets of the contemporary underworld. From the reign of Charles II the face of London changed dramatically with the 1666 fire which burned out the heart of London. Even the south bank was damaged as sparks leaped the water. Wren redesigned The City. Entertainment moved north across the river as theatres, now semi-respectable, were established within The City mile, permitted safer, easier access by the public. Gentlemen founded gambling clubs where they lost fortunes and indulged their appetites in comfort, no longer having to run the gauntlet of seedy locales, pick-pockets and footpads. Pleasures south of the river were left to its residents and it was mostly business carried the wealthy to its shores. Dickens' nineteenth-century London Oliver Twist, Fagin's den was set in the vicinity of notorious Jacob's Island at Bermondsey.

By the eighteenth century at the peak of foreign goods imported, the river was so congested with ships it was possible to walk from one bank to the other across their decks. Vessel damage was frequent due to overcrowding and lack of manoeuvring room. Small boats were unable to get through the ship jam to ply their trade. Owners lost money as cargoes remained undischarged. Ships were forced to waste weeks in idleness while perishables rotted in holds and owners lost buyers to fleeter, more fortunate competitors. To solve the situation, land was acquired and vast complex of docks was built both sides of the river. Northside was St Katherine's, London Docks, Shadwell, Millwall, West and East India, Blackwall, Poplar, The Royal, Dagenham and Tilbury Docks. Southside was St Saviour's, the vast Rotherhithe Surrey Commercial complex; Deptford and Greenwich were refurbished. Shipping and cargoes became efficiently organised. The City and southbank thrived on newly generated wealth although satisfaction was tempered by huge losses sustained through theft. Pepys reckoned as much as seventy percent was lost from cargoes. His measures, including the enclosure of dock areas by high walls, reduced losses to forty percent.

The docks thrived through to the early 1960s. The river bustled with traffic, bristling with tall masts as ships brought all manner of goods from across the world. Sail gave way to steam; loudhailers were exchanged for ship's sirens heard from my home in Welling across from the river, especially on New Year's Eve as the siren of every tug, liner and cargo-carrier on the Thames sounded a joyous cacophony of welcome of the New Year. Hays and Butler's wharves unshipped tea from India, sugar from Barbados, fruit, raisins, spices, oils and meat; all sailed upriver on the tides, discharging at crowded wharves. Regular shiploads of bones arrived from Africa to be boiled into glue and soap. These included skeletons and skulls of lions, tigers, giraffes and other exotic beasts. Nor was it uncommon for dockers to lift a heap of bones to find curled or coiled among them the odd deadly spider or snake. Evocative names of the times remain: Cinnamon Street, Jamaica Road, Cathay Street, Orange Place, Tiger Bay, Greenland

Docks and Shad Thames. The Second World War brought destruction to Thames docklands. Fires raged as ships and docks became prime, easily identifiable targets for enemy bombers. Island Britain relied on its Merchants Navy to get supplies from abroad. The docks were essential for bringing food to the people. Surrey Docks were ablaze for weeks as closely stacked timber burned after a series of raids. A bombed railway arch collapsed killing hundreds of people sheltering beneath it. Shops, factories and rows of houses disappeared as incendiaries took their toll night after night. Many lost everything they had, even their families. As always in times of deep distress, neighbours supported the less fortunate, sharing what they had. The homeless found shelter with friends or relatives. School playgrounds sported brick and concrete air-raid shelters; those forced to wear gasmasks as children still remember the sickly rubber smell and claustrophobic feeling they generated. Everyone conscientiously blacked out their windows, sticking brown tape across them in fancy patterns to combat the effect of bomb-shattered glass.

Once peace was declared attempts were made to clear bomb sites and rebuild. Money was short and many areas were left devastated for years to come. Prefabricated houses, built as temporary accommodation, provided for many homeless. Some made do with partly-demolished or deserted houses, where the owners had moved to the country for safety or found jobs and accommodation out of London. Many emigrated to Commonwealth countries which were quick to offer opportunities to those willing to start a new life abroad. My own parents were ten pound emigrants to Australia in the 1950s while I, as a child, went free. The Festival of Britain celebrating the end of the Second World War encouraged a resurgence of investment in the Arts which now moved back south across the river. Fashionable venues of modern culture such as the Royal Festival Hall, Queen Elizabeth Hall, Purcell room, Hayes Gallery and, later, the National Theatre were erected. In the last decade of the twentieth century, Shakespeare's Globe theatre has been rebuilt close to its original site, thanks to American Sam Wannamaker. Conversion of wharfside warehouses to fashionable apartments is well under way while former wasteground transform into modern, leafy lined estates. The down side of this is that many wharves and dock complexes are now unavailable for their intended purpose. New buildings are built so close to the water's edge the river foreshore is unavailable for general access to the river frontage. It will be interesting to see, in future years, if South Londoners oppose this infringement of their rights.

Each district has its own special ambiance. Bermondsey and Rotherhithe, once thriving working areas dominated by the Surrey Docks and home to thousands of dockers, stevedores and watermen, now tolerates an uneasy alliance with ex-City dwellers anxious to take up newly built or renovated once-derelict riverside buildings; now luxurious accommodation with enviable river views. In the 1980s many were over-priced and snapped up by Yuppies; young, upwardly progressive business people with high salaries and matching life-styles. Deptford's proud history of shipbuilding and fleet victualling is nearly forgotten today. Christopher Marlowe, renowned Elizabethan playwright and suspected spy to Walsingham, was murdered in a rough waterside inn here. Nowdays, the heart of the town is its thriving, bustling market whose stallholders keep up the old traditions and warm friendliness for which it has always been known. I was told of two houses with interconnecting cellars and a secret passage leading down to the waterside for the owner's use, and suspected of being used for smuggling at one time. In contrast, Greenwich, a cut above its more down-to-earth neighbours due to centuries of connections with royalty, deteriorates in faded grandeur despite being a popular tourist attraction. Dreadnought Seamans' Hospital crumbles for lack of official interest, magnificent former Greenwich Hospital, now the Royal Naval College, awaits its fate and currently there is serious consideration of destroying Georgian premises close to the town centre to make way for a new rail terminal. A town which has already had its heart cut from it is Woolwich, once home to The Arsenal built by Henry VIII to store naval munitions, after which The Gunners' famous football team is named. Once a thriving, important place with an array of good class shops and an efficient bus service through its centre to rival any small town, Woolwich now declines into a piece-meal hotchpotch of pedestrianised trader-style marts. Charlton, supporting a resurgent

Charlton Athletic football club, lost its river frontage to modern warehousing. Where wildfowlers once hunted and mudlarkers delved for treasures along its shore stands Thamesmead, a modern self-sufficient concrete town somewhat isolated across former marshland. Once a village of fashionable villas and busy deepwater anchorage with two active yacht clubs, Erith is now largely industrialised but retains its historic associations. Those living on the southern banks of the Thames formed tightly-knit communities, the strength and fierce pride of which can still be felt today. Here are the childhood homes of Michael Caine, Max Bygraves, Tommy Steel, Harry Bowling, Henry Cooper: Bermondsey boys who made it to the top.

Dominant to this whole area is the river, which remains a socially divisive liquid line drawn through the city. It not only exerts a fascination on visitors, but is part of the heart of its people. Pride, nostalgia and an enduring camaraderie for their own runs deep. Scratch any South Londoner and the Thames flows out with his blood: to some, it is essential to their being. Those who move away look back at their lives there with deep affection. But for those who love and know it well the River is dying. Ferries and wherries, once bustling along the water in the hundreds, no longer ply to carry passengers across the water. There is a regular tourist service from Greenwich to Westminster and beyond, a free vehicle and pedestrian ferry at Woolwich, others near Gravesend and Tilbury and a few smaller enterprises but sadly this pleasant form of transport is mainly fading out. Even popular pleasure boats still make trips to Hampton Court and can be hired privately. Royal Naval vessels occasionally moor near HMS *Belfast*, tall ships snuggle into St Katherine's Dock over the river and a few copper-coloured sails billow bravely from masts of mostly privately owned Thames barges. River trade is now mainly downriver at Convoy's Wharf, Deptford, Barking Creek, Dagenham and Tilbury docks, while chandlers and allied river trades such as Pope & Bond's 700-year-old barge-building yard, Greenwich, are closing down.

In the rail-strike torn 1980s an enterprising River Bus service was started. Watermen looked hopefully for a rejuvenation of river traffic and a recognition of the usefulness of water transportation but, despite its reliability, the service was discontinued for lack of support. This is symptomatic of the Thames malaise. As a working river it is woefully under-used compared with European rivers where heavy or bulky commodities are transported by water as matter of course rather than adding to congestion, pollution and deterioration of roads. Multi-skilled rivermen rue it is they who must stay idle as millions of pounds are set aside for new highways requiring acquisition of premium land sites across already overcrowded south London while that other already established massive highway, the river, winds listless and neglected down to the sea with hardly a boat or ship to ripple its surface. With many docks permanently re-assigned and approach roads no longer accessible the hoped-for regeneration of life in river trades may be forlorn. Expertise still readily available is dying and opportunities for alleviating an overburdened road transport system may be permanently lost. A case in point is Watermen and Trinity House pilots dwindling to twenty percent of the number of thirty years ago. Meanwhile, the face of the Thames changes for ever. Future investors recognising our under-use of a valuable resource will need to surmount the problem of much of the riverside having been sold off to private enterprise. Any sizeable dock complex would have to be built east of Woolwich as few wharves are available for their original use. It is ironic that, having generated millions to bring industry to Canary Wharf and the newspaper world at Wapping, valuable assets such as the docks should be sold for a mess of pottage, wiping out a potentially lucrative industry at a stroke.

Meanwhile the river flows on, and with it our reminiscences. This is the river we remember and love, where fish and chips and eel pies could be bought at the corner shop, children swarm as nature intended off Cherry Garden Pier and along the river, five Woodbines or packet of Weights didn't stretch the bank beyond a few pence, while a dockers' toke was a couple of 'doorsteps', a slice of homemade apple pie and a billy of hot tea set aside ready with his cap and muffler by his missis before he went off to be called on by the day. It is a changed world.

One

Tower Bridge

The Thames has twenty-eight bridges. The first to be built, London Bridge, designed by Brother Peter, of St Mary Colchurch, was completed 1209. The latest is Dartford's Queen Elizabeth II. By the mid-1800 the City Corporation Select Committee found increased dock traffic urgently needed a bridge across Lomdon's Pool. Main design considerations were for normal passage of both pedestrians and vehicles, as well as permitting the bigger ships through to the Upper Pool as required; quite a tall order. Some submitted designs were weird and wonderful; an elaborate tunnel on the river bed to a skyscraper incorporating hydraulic lifts. The accepted plan, October 1844, was redesigned on earlier plan by City architect Horace Jones and John Wolfe Barry incorporated modern hydraulic technology to lift two massive steel and iron bascules each weighing 950 tons, pivoting from the base of two 206ft high baronial gothic towers, 200ft apart, and embedded in concrete-filled caissons to a depth of 46ft. The two towers were to be held together by a combination of iron suspension 'ropes' and rigid girders forming two overhead walkways 142 ft above the Thames at high tide; the design visually complement the nearby Tower of London, were borne by Bridge House Estates out of it original investment in the first London Bridge. Jones died soon after construction began. His young assistant, John Stephenson, took over. Sir William Arrol was given the basic steel and iron structure contract, making and shipping the main towers from Scotland. The hydraulically-powered engines generating 760 psi were designed by William Armstrong, while the task of cladding the structure in Portland stone and Cornish granite was awarded to Perry Company. Estimated costs were £750,000 but finally cost £1,000,000. The Prince of Wales laid the foundation stone on 21 June 1876. There was public animosity to the stark steel structure slowly taking shape but once the stone cladding was started by Perry's aversion turned to admiration. The Bridge was opened by the Prince and Princess of Wales on 30 June 1894. A multitude lined the river banks to witness the ceremony. The Pool was crowded with sightseers in all manner of hired boats, while road and river traffic halted for the great occasion as their Royal Highnesses' carriage drove both ways across the bridge to mark its official opening. As the Prince turned a uniquely designed silver stirrup cup to officially raise the bascules for the first time a cacophony of saluting cannons and trumpets, cheers from the crowd and blasts of jubilation from ships' whistles and sirens reverberated across the water. Tower Bridge continues to thrill. In its first year the bascules were operated over 6,000 times, in the 1930s, 7,500 times a year and in the river's busiest period, 1950s, they were operated 9,000 times annually; speed limit was 20mph. Nowadays the bridge opens a mere 500 times a year. Operating costs are borne by the Fund. The hydraulic lifting gear was in continuous use, until converted to cheaper electric power in 1976. Advance application (24 hours) must be made for raising the bridge but there is no charge. Once, ships notified Cherry Garden Pier who passed their request to the Bridgemaster, presently Keith Patterson. In the red brick engine house, now The Tower Bridge Experience, visitors are shown original hydraulic lifting gear, still in efficient working order after 100 years of use, and can brave the overhead walkways 142 ft over the river. Mrs J. Lavinia Easter's father, William John Follows, born 1900, worked on the bridge as a driver from 5 January 1931 before entering the navy in 1939. She recalls frequent visits to her father with her two sisters, and seeing the bridge brasswork 'gleaming as if it was an ornament'.

With his Company's team of experts masons Sir Herbert Bartlett's talents are literally clad in stone. Philatropist and an essentially private man who liked to eat alone, he played a large part in financing Sir Ernest Shackleton's South Pole expedition, where a mountain was named in his honour. As Commodore of Royal London Y.C. he moored his schooner in the Thames and donated the original 4ft high solid silver cup for the Americas Race. Having to withdraw at the last minute from officiating at an event in Hardington Mandeville, Somerset, he donated the princely sum of £100 to the village by way of apology: the Council gratefully used this for replacement church bells, cast at Bow and still in use, inscribed with Sir Herbert's name.

Sir Herbert owned Perry & Co, stonemasons, and was ultimately responsible for the beauty of Tower Bridge's stonework. Jones had originally intended the two towers to be of red brick, conforming to Victorian Gothic in the manner of St Pancras. His successor, John Stephenson, insisted on stone as being more in keeping with nearby Tower of London. Sir Herbert Bartlett found the ideal stone for the job, raising a monument which Londoners immediately took to their own. Sir Herbert was a guest at the original ceremony and banquet to mark the opening of the bridge and on 30 June 1994 his great grandson, Sir John, was invited to the Centenary banquet where he was presented with a leather-bound commemorative book, graciously signed by Prince Charles to mark the occasion.

Alfred Wheatley snr. was head stonemason for Perry & Co. His work was held in such high regard that he was made a unique presentation at the completion of Tower Bridge. Mr Wheatley had a most unfortunate death, dying of ptomaine poisoning five year's after the completion of the bridge. He had no sense of smell or taste so was unable to detect anything amiss with food. Unfortunately hygiene was often lacking in the nineteenth century. One evening while at a restaurant, fellow diners warned, 'Don't touch the meat, it's bad.' He said, 'Rubbish, I'm hungry!' ate it and died. He is buried in Richmond cemetery.

Alfred Jesse Wheatley jnr., Alfred Henry's son, worked under his father at Perry's and was also involved in the construction of the Bridge.

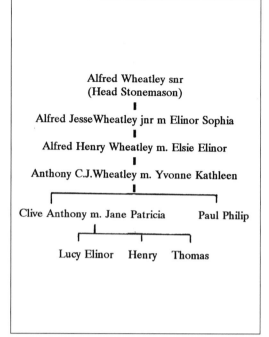

Alfred Wheatley snr
(Head Stonemason)

Alfred Jesse Wheatley jnr m Elinor Sophia

Alfred Henry Wheatley m. Elsie Elinor

Anthony C.J. Wheatley m. Yvonne Kathleen

Clive Anthony m. Jane Patricia   Paul Philip

Lucy Elinor   Henry   Thomas

Mr H.H. Bartlett, later Sir Herbert, owner of Perry & Co., wrote this testimonial to Mr Albert Wheatley, Head Stonemason and Foreman.

Trafalgar Works
Bow
London July 13 1894

Perry & Co
Builders & Contractors
Telephone No 5417
Telegraphic Address
'Utility London'

Dear Wheatley,
        I have the pleasure to enclose cheque and at the same time to express to you my thanks and appreciation of the masterly and highly satisfactory manner in which you have completed your last job viz the Tower Bridge which is a fitting climax to a career of splendid help and absolute integrity.
        You have well earned a repose and I cannot dissuade you from taking it knowing as I do that such was your wish before you entered upon this last work which will stand to your credit forever.
        I hope you will accept some souvenir from me to remind you of my personal regard and estime and if I can ever be of any service to you it will give me great pleasure. I shall miss you very much, it will be a parting I will feel deeply. I shall always look back upon the time of our connection and work together with pleasant memories of you. I wish you health and long life.
        I remain
        Yours very faithfully,
        H. H. Bartlett
P.S. Of course our money matters are not yet closed Take such holidays as you wish.

Four generations of the Wheatley family, clockwise: Elinor, Tony, Janet and Henry.

FRED KARNO's ARMY

The nickname of the newly-raised WW I British Army was an allusion to the comedian and stage burlesque by Fred "Karno" John Westcott who died in 1914. Like Karno's motley stage gear, the newly conscripted, untrained British soldiers were issued ill fitting, ill matched uniforms. The well-known army chorus, sung to the tune of "The church's one foundation" runs :

"We are Fred Karno's army,
Fred Karno's infantry:
We cannot fight, we cannot shoot
So what damn good are we ?
But when we get to Berlin
The Kaiser he will say
'Hoch, hoch, mein Gott
Vot a bloody fine lot,
Fred Karno's infantry,'"

In WW II "Old Hitler" was substituted for "the Kaiser".

EH

During the Second World War, E.F. Cato Carter's unit was stationed on Tower Bridge to guard it from the enemy. Apart from cold nights, noisy air-raids and military duties not much occured during his tour. He was fortunate to miss the night a 'doodlebug' hit the overhead walkway, bounced off onto the Tower's tug boat moored below and sank her with her crew. After the war Mr Carter was a loss adjuster at the docks for the government. There was so much bomb damage that claims were compassionately settled almost without question to enable business to resume as quickly as possible.

Tower Bridge's tug, *Sunshine* waits to be called out on duty in the 1930s. Powerful-engined *Sun* tugs still work the river, helping to berth, reverse, pull away or turn any ship which needs their services.

There was great excitement on the Thames in May, 1949 when the newly designed Short Solent flying boat flew up river, landed at Greenwich Reach towards Tower Bridge before taxiing beneath raised bascules into the Upper Pool to moor alongside Tower Wharf. Weighing 35 tons with twin decks and seating 39 passengers, the Solent was the biggest commercial aircraft of its day. At a ceremony five days later Sir George Aylwen, Lord Mayor of London, named her *City of London*. MPTD

Twenty years after the *City of London* landed, a small monoplane, having insufficient power to fly above Tower Bridge, was forced to manoeuvre through the arch on its way upriver. The few unwitting, startled witnesses standing on the bridge must have ducked sharply as the aircraft flew close overhead. MPTD

Pay and conditions not being what they are today, a 1930s representative boatload of Merchant Navy officers sailed up the Thames to petition parliament for better standards and wages. Unlike the royal yacht of today, their small boat, the *Brittania*, did not require the bridgemaster to raise Tower Bridge's bascules as they sailed up to Westminster. PLA

The destroyer, HMS *Gloucester*, heads to Hanover Hole between Thames Tunnel Mills and Wapping police station after being backed through Tower Bridge by two tugs, *Sun Thames* forward and *Sun Anglia* aft.

'If you can't afford a day at Margate it is sometimes just as much fun making do with what you have on your doorstep. On a hot day in 1930 what better than a family outing to the shore beside Tower Bridge to make mud-and-sand pies in the warm sunshine. Some of us took off our shoes, others still had our hair in curlers and scarves knotted on top. Dad had the day off but still kept his shoes on and Mum wouldn't be parted from her apron. Some children wore posh sundresses and hats but most swam in the altogether or just paddled. The old coal shovel did just as well as a sand spade and pushchairs made handy seats when you wanted a natter with friends and neighbours. Someone even brought one of those Japanese parasols: maybe they got it cheap from a totter.' PLA

Waterman Len Coker has taken part in many river races, but he was content to photograph and admire the tall ships' race of 1980. Tower Bridge raises her bascules in salute to the grace of a byegone age when a three-masted sailing ship barely clears the 142ft high span of the overhead walkways as she glides into the Lower Pool. Sailing ships come from the continent, Australia, New Zealand and America to take part in this prestigous race and retired sailing men look with nostalgia at their passing.

In the morning sunshine three work boats head off to work down river. Tower Bridge has been a silent and dignified witness to all the tides of fortune : the rags to riches of society; the rise and fall of river-borne trade; the success, dignity and eventual humbling of long established river associated businesses and the over-all pride of fair pay for a good day's work done. While remaining a strong attraction to anyone visiting London, Tower Bridge remains a major part of all that makes the Thames dear to the hearts of those who live and work along its shores. When dignitaries lay foundation stones to new buildings the silver spade they use is suitably inscribed and kept in a glass case. So what happened to the mallet used to put the last stone into place when Tower Bridge was completed? You'll have to ask the proud possessor, Ted Callan.

Two
River Pilots

There are two types of pilots on the Thames: Waterman pilots and PLA Trinity House pilots. Both do similar jobs but PLA pilots are Master Mariners and their river territory extends further than that of Waterman pilots who are licensed by the Company of Watermen and Lightermen to work on the river and in dock areas. Once Trinity House men were divided into river and sea-going pilots, the two changing posts at Gravesend. Now the changeover point may be Crayford Ness, Long Reach, Purfleet or Barking Creek and an incoming PLA man may take a ship right up to The Pool and into dock, but (not out of it). Watermen pilots have always had limited territory and have no official authorization for what they do, although they are, and have to be, licensed to carry out their job: under the 1913 Pilotage Act, Watermen are 'recognised' as 'a type of person' to shift vessels for a distance of two nautical miles, or for any distance west of Barking Creek. They can also shift any kind of vessel inside enclosed docks; tricky work requiring the ability to manoeuvre large vessels in restricted spaces among other, usually stationary vessels. A pilot is on board ship in the capacity of expert advisor to the Captain of a vessel wishing to sail to or from a berth. Navigating a river, possibly for the first time, can be a tricky business so pilots are normally welcome aboard. However, Captains remain in charge of their ships at all times and may prefer to make their own decisions, such as not wanting to use tugs to turn a vessel or taking a bend at a speed different to that recommended by the pilot: that choice is his prerogative. The pilot will hand control of the vessel back to a Captain if his advice is being over-ridden. Such expertise takes years of learning a river's idiosyncracies, tides and hazards as well as navigational skills, so pilot's much sought-after licences are hard-earned. Commander Mike 'John' Cooley, a Master Mariner licensed by the Ministry of Transport, has piloted on the Thames for thirty years. Originally training as Naval gunnery officer on a type 15 Frigate, 'long since gone', he was active in amphibious warfare. He retired as Commander, RNR, with an appointment with the Ministry of Defence, later becoming a Trinity House Pilot now under the PLA. He handles many types of vessel including RN ships such as the famous battle cruiser, HMS Belfast, destroyers like HMS Gloucester, the royal yacht Britannia (22 times) and cargo ships.

As a young man Peter Sargent became an apprenticed waterman and lighterman. For this, he attended Waterman's Hall, St Mary-At-Hill, London. His swearing-in ceremony to the Worshipful Company of Freemen of the River Thames indentured him under the professional eye of his father, Leslie, who now also become his Master, before the august company of be-robed, fur-trimmed Master Barge Owners. Starting from scratch as a deckhand, Pete learned to handle all types of vessel from barges to sea-going cargo ships and tankers. Seven years later, on completion of apprenticeship, he returned to Waterman's Hall to receive his Freedom of the River, having learned by practical application the ways of the waters of the Thames and its tributaries as well as his own road. Having seen both Trinity House and Waterman pilots in action one can only marvel at their expertise and skills. Turning a 50,000 tons, 700ft vessel in its own length midstream at either Hanover Hole or Barking Creek is a sight to behold; few veteran rivermen resist watching such demonstrations of skill. Judged by eighteenth century laws today's pilots have it easy: then, 'By the laws of Oleron, if (the pilot's) fault is notoriously gross, that the ship's crew sees an apparent wreck, they may lead him to the hatches and strike off his head.' By the laws of Denmark 'an ignorant pilot is to pass thrice under the ship's keel' – as good as a death sentence. No wonder they learned their job so well!

The tug *Sun Thames* preparing to take the strain, ready to pull HMS *Gloucester* away from HMS *Belfast* in the Upper Pool. A furled sailed barge bobs sedately at a nearby jetty.

Mooring a ship is a complex business as ropes have to be secured corresponding to the strain being put on a ship according to the tide and type of berth. The mooring winches on *Gefion*'s forward deck cover most requirements. The life of a river pilot is ruled by the tides. Turning a ship around that bit faster can make the difference between a prompt departure or double the anchorage fees for the shipping company if a tide is missed.

'Fit's like a glove!' The pilot of *S.S.Mauretania* slid her sharp bows neatly into dock in 1939 as dockside is crowded with sightseers. The three tugs which guided her to the entrance can be seen astern. Two port and starboard lines have been thrown ashore and secured. Her starboard deck rails are crowded as crew members watch her progress into dock. A pilot cannot make his mistakes in private: should he make a error there are usually more than a few witnesses only to eager to comment on it. PLA

Trinity House pilots after an official ceremony with the *Oswestry Grange* around 1940. PLA

The *Sea Rhone*, in from Holland, taken up Barking Creek by Pete Sargent. In the doorway, watchful for his ship is the captain, Enzio, born in Italy and living in Croatia. His First Officer, Mario, is Croatian. Their cargo of steel coils was speedily unloaded to allow *Sea Rhone* to catch the outgoing tide.

Left: The royal yacht *Britannia* being piloted down the Thames by Mike Cooley around 1982. Erith applied to have *Britannia* moored at their deepwater jetty on retirement from service in 1997. Right: With two mooring lines already unfastened and one to go, Pete and Dave Sargent, father and son, work together to release the *Irene* ready to be piloted back down the Thames. Piloting depends upon the tides so can never be a 9 'til 5 job.

The *Formidable* is one of the largest tugs on the Thames today. Working under instructions from the pilot, she manoeuvres towards the *Irene*'s newly released port side ropes ready to make them fast to her stern. Behind her can be seen the shoreline of Thamesmead.

Pilots cannot always board a ship by means of a gangway. Sometimes they have to meet a boat mid-river and board it while she is still making way. Mounting or descending a ship's side by rope ladder as high as a house is all part of the pilot's day's work. Extended rungs allow two people to pass each other and also prevent the ladder twisting while it is being climbed.

Charlie, John and Jim ready to release the *Irene* from her moorings. A VHF radio allows communication between the pilot, watermen, tug master and ship's captain.

Sometimes there is no room to use tugs in turning a ship. If the terrain allows it she can be 'bulrushed'. Hardly disturbing the ducks at their feeding, *Marinier*'s nose has been driven forward into the reeds and mud. The flow of the tide is then utilised to swing her stern upriver. When she nearly faces the direction she is to go, bow thrust engines back her off the mud and she is under way.

Even today the river can be a crowded place with craft of all types needing to find their space. To help minimise accidents all who sail the river must learn the thirty-one articles of regulations. No mariner may take control of a ship unless he has mastered these. Some rules are made simple: Green to green, or red to red means perfect safety, go ahead; if to your starboard red appear, it's your duty to keep clear; when both lights you see ahead – starboard wheel and show your red. Whistles and sirens are also used for signalling: 1 short blast means 'I am going to starboard'; 2 short blasts mean 'I am going to port'; 3 short blasts mean 'I am going full speed astern'. In fog, a vessel under way sounds one long blast at two-minute intervals. A steam vessel under way, but stationery in the water, sounds two blasts at two-minute intervals.

Piloting ships into dock or sea-going barges down twisting creek channels calls for expertise, especially where a barge's length obstructs the view or the vessel is about 800ft long. Car drivers unable to 3-point-turn a 15ft x 5ft car in roads 25ft wide could learn a thing or two here. A lock width may allow only inches to spare either side. 'You're not expected to touch land at all and they look at you as if you're an idiot if you do' recalls Mike Cooley. 'I remember going in once and the dock master said "You're not allowed to touch there!" This was on the radio, so I said "Just run round and push her off, there's a good chap."' Downriver from Tower Bridge is Hanover Hole: a deep part of the river since the close piers of Mediaeval London Bridge obstructed tidal flow. Here, and at Greenwich, heavy tonnage ships have sufficient depth to turn in their own length with the help of pilots and tugs. Trinity House pilots, self-employed under charter from Henry VIII, were confered the privilege of wearing naval uniform when they rafted the Thames with available boats to prevent Admiral Tromp's Dutch fleet sailing up to take London after defeating the British at the river's estuary 10 December, 1652. Originally Trinity House issued their pilot licenses and kept accounts; pilots found their own jobs. In 1988 the government decreed the PLA responsible for the 1,500 Trinity House pilots, who were still deemed self-employed, but ports could contract-out their jobs to someone else. Under legal advice they opted to become employees of the port authorities to safeguard their rights. Today, there are a mere 150 PLA pilots and about twenty waterman pilots left for the dwindling river trade.

Three
Bermondsey and Rotherhithe

The Hay's, Butler's and Braithwaite & Deanwere part of Bermondsey. There were docks at St Saviour's and Dockhead, between Shad Thames and Mill Street. Surrey Commercial Docks covered Rotherhithe peninsular from the Tunnel Mills along Limehouse Reach and comprised Albion, Canada, Greenland, Island, Lavender, Nelson, Russia, Quebec, South and Stave Docks, Central and Globe Ponds and Surrey Basin. Nell Richardson lived in Bermondsey. Her mother came over from Dublin where she was born near the coastguard station. On 31 August 1939, three days before war started, Nell married Charlie Griffin at Bermondsey Town Hall before their wedding at the church in Paradise Street. She was one of thirteen children.

Sidney Fagan, last of a long line of watermen, writes 'In the late 1920s, aged about nine, I often jumped on tailboards of lorries for free rides to Tower Bridge. I'd walk down the nearby granite steps, then along Shad Thames: a narrow thoroughfare running alongside the inlet of St Saviour's Dock with wharves on both its banks. Passing under overhead bridges connecting wharves on either side I'd savour aromas from Courage's brewery – barley, malt and hops; floury smells from various wharves and, at one wharf in summer seasons, the bitter aroma of Seville oranges destined for our local marmalade factory. Cloth-capped men at loopholes used wall cranes to lower wooden crates or sets of bulging sacks to carts or lorries waiting below. I'd often stop at some river steps to watch the bascules of Tower Bridge which rose about a dozen times a day for ships to enter or leave the Upper Pool. At the end of Shad Thames I went round by Dockhead, along Mill Street, smelling the dog biscuits made in nearby Spiller's factory, then along Bermondsey Wall. This was, perhaps, the favourite part of my walks, with smells of raisins, currants and sultanas mingling with a rich variety of spicy aromas such as nutmeg and cinnamon. From Cherry Garden Pier I watched passing barges, rowed by lightermen using sweeps 28 feet long; yellow or red-funnelled tugs towed pair-bridled barges, often in sixes. Sometimes mud-dredgers or huge floating cranes were towed by at a snail's pace. At low tide flat-bottomed barges sprawled on the foreshore like huge, dead frogs. Around them were layers of thick, grey custard-like mud exuding a strong, pungent odour. Small, swift Dutch coasters moored up at nearby wharves. Cranes swung high and low either side of the river like tall, feeding giraffes. Sometimes I climbed onto Platform Wharf near the Angel public house with its wooden verandah overlooking the river. Too poor to afford costumes, we swam from here during summer holidays wearing only birthday suits while keeping watch for Wapping police launches likely to shoot across river to chase us away: so many boys drowned during the holidays it was a cause for concern. In 1926 Len, my older brother, then apprentice lighterman, dived off his barge to save a drowning boy and was presented with a Royal Humane Society medal for his bravery. My walks took me to Rotherhithe Street with its barge-building and repair noises. A deafening stutter of rivetting and scary hisses of welding reverberated along the narrow street. Horses and carts racketed along the set-stones, steel-rimmed wheels striking granite kerbs to give off fireworks of sparks. Occasionally I saw a lighterman carrying his harpoon-like hitcher over one shoulder: these were used to 'poke' or push barges about in non-tidal waters in docks, canals or in slack water. By Rotherhithe Gasworks was the stench of coke and sulphur. If the wind was westerly, the smell of softwood timber came from nearby Surrey Commercial Docks. Jamaica Road took me home again after a wonderfully satfisfying feast of rich aromas.'

Ships berthing in Rotherhithe entered into the community in more ways than one. Just missing the rooftop of a nearby fruitshop, the bowsprit of this ship makes a handy spot for sailors to order a basketful of groceries from a nearby shopkeeper. With no television to watch and radio still only at the primitive 'cat's whisker' stage, sailors' tales of voyages would be eagerly awaited and earn the teller his welcome pint in the local pub. PLA

Sidney and mother, Mrs Fagan were happy living in Keetons Road, Bermondsey. During the war nearby houses and the school were bombed but their house escaped damage. Sidney, from a long line of lightermen and watermen, broke the family mould by becoming a teacher after leaving the army. Taking part in the Normany invasion convinced him of the evils of war.

In 1956 Sidney, aged 37, taught Junior Class 1, Sandhurst Road School, Catford, all fondly remembered are: J.Deanville, K.Brown, R.Someville, R.Linenden, A.Bush, D.Prior, C.Dryland, P.Harper, G. Billin, Alex Homes, Philip Hawley, M.Baines, N.Allan, C.Kinard, P.Kitonytas, D.Plowright, V.Jerome, G.Boulkes, S.Waller, M.Cartwright, I.Lemkin, R.Mellish, J.Reowill, P.Tyler, J. Selby, J.Crook, Mr Fagan, D.Dicks, J.P. Smith, R.Morris, E.Ivory, D.Stanton, R.Rooke, G.Herbert, R.Wayne, B.Barrett, P.Richardson, D.Plumer, I.Maxted.

Visits to the seaside were a rare treat and in 1927 Mrs Gore took Sidney, aged 8 (left), his cousin Stanley, and her son George to Canvey Island for the day and my, wasn't the water cold!

Docks were mysterious places and great for a child to explore. St Saviour's was no exception. While no-one was looking, adventurous boys could nip into all sorts of secret hidey holes and not be found until teatime. Each wharf had a winch above the column of waterside doors, and each doorway had chain-held landing flaps for lowering to receive cargo being winched up from barges in the dock below.

By 1973 Sidney Fagan was teaching at Alderwood School, Eltham. A popular class story was Clive King's, 'Stig of the Dump': Sidney invited Clive to school so the children could meet him. Eagerly waiting to ask questions are Paula Rooks, Beverley Jones, Paul Bryan, Joseph Brooks on Clive King's right. Sidney keeps a friendly eye from behind on Paul, Stuart Mair, Paula Slavin and Jenny Williams.

Peek Freans, biscuit manufacturers of Bermondsey, presented and maintained a grand slide for local children in the park of St James church, Bermondsey. Peek Freans left Bermondsey some years ago and regular railway commuters lost a useful digital clock, visible from trains running over the Five Hundred Arches. Sadly, says Bill Shrieve, the slide now deteriorates for lack of maintenance.

33

Across from Wapping police station are Rotherhithe and Bermondsey. Surrey Dock entrance was downriver from the Engine House and South Metropolitan Gas Works. Isambard Brunel's twin tunnels, under Tunnel Mills and completed in 1843 after twenty years, were designed for carriages and pedestrians. Charles Dickens' son called it 'relatively useless'. Later it was utilized by the East London Railway. Captain Christopher Jones of *The Mayflower* is buried at St Mary's

When the *S.S. Kolpino* docked at the Surrey Commercial in January 1964 dockers were surprised to see a camel aboard. He was part of an assignment of animals from Moscow Zoo which included five camels, one reindeer, one wild ass, six ibex and seven antelopes. One camel looks as if his comments on his reception and our British weather were not at all favourable. PLA

church. Old wharves have gone and the tall spar-makers house now stands alone near King's Stairs. Wartime River Emergency Service met in the seventeenth-century Angel riverside pub near old Bermondsey police station. Watermen still meet here after work. Braithwaite and Dean, barge repairers were upriver from the pub.

Only a stone's throw from Tower Bridge was Butler's Wharf, among the busiest in London. Their warehouses were at Horsleydown and Shad Thames. Known as the Larder of London, Butlers traded in tea, coffee, spices and dried fruits among other commodities. Their largest warehouses were near Tower Bridge on the south bank. These have recently been converted to contain the Design Museum. PLA

The river frontage at Rotherhithe was a bustling, thriving melée of companies, large and small, connected with the business of supplying London and England with every kind of commodity from abroad. Along the waterfront were names to conjure memories: Pocock's, barge builders, G. Pace rented out barges. Braithwaite and Dean, one of the larger barge suppliers who owned several premises, must have been good employers as ex-watermen speak well of them. PLA

The oldest pubs along the Bermondsey-Rotherhithe riverfront are The Mayflower (formerly Spread Eagle and Crown), The Angel and The Grapes, a small, bow-fronted building with flying buttress chimney pictured here in 1970. Brunel's navvies patronised The Spread Eagle when building the Thames Tunnel.

The building of Surrey Docks began in the second half of the nineteenth century. In 1870 Canada Dock was built by Lang & Aird. It looks as if sailing ships were already queuing at the gates ready to be let in on completion. PLA

The Port of London Authority took control of the Surrey Commercial and other docks in 1909. Dockmasters held positions of great responsibility. In 1909, when the PLA were due to takeover, the dockmasters' staff assembled aboard their SCD Co. tug, *Canada* for a rare photograph together. Moustaches were definitely in vogue at that time. PLA

Between and after the Second World War most of our citrus fruit, bananas, lamb, wool, butter, wheat and cheese came from the Commonwealth. Cheeses were packed in slatted wooden barrels or crates to allow them to 'breathe' in transit. The long line of porters trucking cheeses from quayside to warehouse is a sight no longer seen today. Jackie Vaughan's dad (now ninety) worked as a Hays Wharf docker for forty years, as did most of his brothers and his son. PLA

Many dockers and stevedores relied on the open call system, arriving in the early morning at a dock's gates for the dockmaster to call on men required for a day's work. The lucky ones got jobs lasting several days or weeks: others got nothing. Surrey Docks' call was at Redriff Road near the swing bridge. Some dockers worked regularly for a Freeman who found them reliable. Ted Callan could expect to get a message from his Freeman the night before a job which may require getting up at 0400 with barely time for a couple of slices of 'holy ghost' (toast) and a pot of 'rosy lea' before catching a tram to work. PLA

Once whalers hauled into Howlands Wet Dock, later Greenland Passage. Now, it holds lesser fish. Gus Baulch, ex-London docker, remembers ships sailing in from all over the world. One Chinese vessel docked with a cargo of pottery and koi carp. In 1950 the English did not set as much store by these fancy fish as today, so when customs officers refused to allow the carp ashore the captain ordered them tipped into the dock. I was assured they are still there to this day, ready to feature in some fisherman's tall tale.

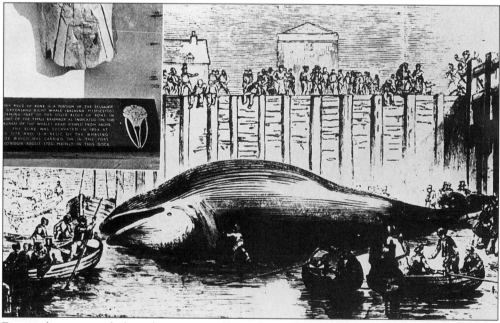

Eigteenth-century whaling ships, too small to take a whale on board once harpooned, lashed them to the ship's side to float into dock. Whaling stations had large steel slipways up which carcasses were winched onto steel flenging decks. Curved, keenly honed flenging knives cut the blubber into manageable chunks which were cast into deep steel boiling chambers set into the deck. No signs of such arrangements have been found at Greenlands within living memory although a skull of a whale was unearthed in 1954. PLA

Large ships in for repairs put into dry dock such as Nelson Dock at Rotherhithe. Ships sailed in at high tide under the shadow of St Mary's church, were propped into position, closed off from the river and left 'high and dry' when the tide went out, enabling necessary work to be done clear of the water, as in this 1815 etching. PLA

A small yacht can easily be hauled onto a slipway, lifted into an adapted barge or raised out of the water by sling hoist, as was this 20-footer at Greenland Dock, complete with an over 30ft mast. Dry docking has always been an expensive business, no matter how it is achieved but without maintenance craft would not stay in good shape for long. Wooden vessels are attacked marine worms eating the planking. Iron ships suffer from rust. Concrete barges crumble as they develop cracks, while fibre glass boats are subject to porousness due to osmosis.

Watermen need patience. Water in a dock is maintained at a high level controlled by lock gates. It is uneconomical to 'lock in' or out just a few boats so there have to be several vessels ready to use it before the lock is operated. This takes time, depending on individual locks. Vessels are released according to draft, those requiring deeper water having to wait until last. These sailing barges were ready to sail back into the river from Surrey Commerial in 1930. The middle barge in the second row, *Oak*, was built by Howards. PLA

The massive lock gates are still in use at Greenland Passage. They are moved by hydraulic capstans worked by pressure from the tidal Thames. Measurements of tidal rise and fall in feet are visible up the sides of the dock entrance walls. The docks are now mainly used for visiting private craft looking for a brief haven.

Some timbers can be floated, or rafted, without damage. Sometimes it was more economical to transport from ship to shore in this way rather than paying docking fees. Timber lengths were bound together by cross beams and formed into a series of rafts which were fastened together to form a long trail of floating timber. This could then be moved under oars from ship to dock, by one, or sometimes two men. PLA

Sailing across the North Sea, her decks filled to capacity with spruce, the Swedish ship, *Frigg* met rough weather causing her cargo to shift to starboard. Her stern dips beneath the water and her plimsoll mark is sunk without trace as she heels several degrees off the vertical. The latter part of her journey must have been uncomfortable and dangerous for the crew as it would be no mean feat to balance on the wet, steeply sloping deck in heavy seas, not to mention the problem of sleeping in ones bunk if it happened to be on the port side. Despite the problems, *Frigg*'s load did not come adrift. PLA

The greatest commodity handled by the Surrey Commercial Docks was balk and sawn lumber transported from Norway, Canada and other countries. Harry Skelton says that deal porters could accurately stack timber by eye and hands as straight as if they had used a plumb line. They reliably 'sized' wood for length and thickness without a measure. An assorted shipload is discharged at Greenland Dock, 1957. A variety of barges wait to lighten her load. Despite being laden to capacity, just one man could move a fully-loaded barge under oars by a series of tacks or zig-zags to keep on course. Lower Thames is divided into reaches such as Gallions, down to the Nore. A 'reach' is the approximate distance a barge can travel on one tack. PLA

Hot and sweet! Mr Brewster's mugs of tea were welcomed by dock workers when his mobile canteen appeared on dockside at the Surrey Commercial in 1935. PLA

New Zealand lamb has always been prized for its flavour and this consignment, individually wrapped in cheesecloth and stamped with the exporter's name, was welcome in post-war Britain. Each type of cargo was slung according to its needs: spreaders were not needed when lifting rigid, frozen carcasses. PLA

When the 1951 Festival of Britain celebrations were held on South Bank, of which Festival Hall was a part, all that was best in Britain was sent there on exhibition. The locomotive, *London Mammoth* was shipped to the Surrey Docks where it was handled by the PLA for the Festival. PLA

A Courtaulds cargo ship, bristling with derricks and winches, stands ready to discharge crates to the lighter, *Wrekin* in Surrey Docks. As lightermen loaded their own barges it was to their advantage to ensure the cargo was well-balanced when doing so: a heavily-loaded, badly-listing boat was difficult to both steer and move, was a danger to other rivercraft and it wouldn't do to lose the cargo en route. PLA

Gus Baulch remembers when the docks were so crowded a docker could walk with ease across the decks from one side of the dock to the other. A variety of vessels jostled for space around Surrey Dock's station yard in 1920. PLA

Many companies worked the Surrey Docks, each running their own arrangements until unified under the PLA early this century. One such firm was Burt, Boulton & Hayward Ltd, who owned a timber yard. Available staff assembled for a company photo in March 1926, outside their office. The wide variety of neckwear is interesting and a hitcher, or barge hook, is in the front row. PLA

Once there were fifteen large dry docks along the Thames. The Nelson, built in the 1700s, is one of the last. Built for ship building, the dock turned to repair work once northern yards took over the industry. The three-masted vessel docked there was once *La Dame de Serk* but has since become *Traders*.

The graceful *La Dame de Serk* (one of several ways the name can be spelt) was built in 1952 as a French naval training vessel. In the 1970s she was sold for use as a pleasure cruise boat sailing between the isles of Sark and Guernsey but was later sold for scrap. In 1989 Holiday Inn hotels bought her, sailed her to Portsmouth for a complete re-fit as a restaurant and brought her to Nelson Dock, since when she has proved popular as the restaurant Traders Bistro and a great setting for reminiscence parties.

Four
Tug Skipper

Captain Maurice Jones was a PLA tug skipper who worked the river for forty years. Although retired, he still keeps up with current river events such as barge races and meets old river friends. He held both a waterman's and a lighterman's licence. Having served his seven years apprenticeship as a deckhand, mate, engineer and, finally, master, he earned his Freedom of the River. As a PLA pilot he wore a distinctive navy uniform with the Authority's brass buttons and navy-style cap. Maurice has worked in all the major London docks and towed many types of vessel including large cargo ships such as the Imperial Star owned by the Blue Star Line and when he was the captain of the Lord Devonport he towed barges. The PLA had four H 58 tugs, their names all starting with 'PLA': Platina, Playgirl, Plangent and Plato. As with river pilots, tug captains have to know the tides, width, length and depth of the major docks, which arches of the many Thames bridges to use and the compass bearings of different reaches as well as general sailing knowledge, which boils down to the art of ship management and maintenance, and the capacity to use foresight and common sense, to make the fullest use of watermen's experience. When HM King George VI made an official visit to The Royals, Maurice and other senior PLA were priviledged to escort him round the dock complex.

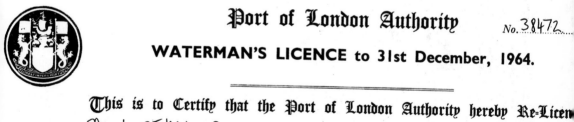

Maurice Jones' Waterman's licence which required annual renewal.

Left: The bridge of a PLA tug was well laid out and surprisingly roomy. Maurice Jones stands with the wood and brass ship's wheel behind the gleaming brass telegraph of *Plangent*. Right: Captain Maurice Jones, skipper of *Plangent*, with *Plangent*'s Mate in Connaught Roads, Albert Dock in the 1960s.

Maurice Jones aboard the tug *Platina* chats with a colleague while awaiting his next job. Behind lies the *Antarctic Queen* at berth. Nowadays most fenders are old tractor or car tyres, but in the 1950s fenders were hand knotted from old ropes or oakum using a succession of wall plait bends.

50

Five

Deptford and Greenwich

Deptford, a corruption of 'deep ford', still has set-stone streets at its centre and many of its old buildings survive, although there are new blocks of flats and most of the old terraced cottages have gone. Diarist Samuel Pepys, naval clerk, well known for his love of gentlemen's pursuits and the theatre, was a frequenter of Deptford, Greenwich, Woolwich and Erith. In his diary entry for 15 January, 1660 Pepys wrote 'The King hath been this afternoon at Deptford, to see the yacht that Commissioner Pett is building, which will be very pretty; as also that his brother at Woolwich is making.' (p.65) Ferry crossings were the usual mode of transport in Pepys' day, and on 5 November he writes 'By water to Deptford, and there made a visit to Mr Evelyn.' A close friend and fellow seventeenth century diarist, John Evelyn, lived at Says Court, Deptford and failed with his brick-making business there: a street and public house are named after him in the area. In his History of the Czar Peter the Great, Emperor of all Russia (printed 'at the Looking-glafs on London-Bridge' in 1740) J. Hodges wrote '...a very neat (house) was fitted up for him at Deptford, where he would often take up the carpenter's Tools, and work with them. Seeing with how nuch more Skill our People worked than the Ship-Builders in Holland, he thought his time mifpent all the Time he was there, and ufed to fay he fhould never have learned his Trade, if he had not come to England.' In the nineteenth century Deptford Corporation bought the site of the abandoned dockyard and converted it into a foreign cattle market where infected stock were removed from ships to be slaughtered. D.W. Richards has vivid memories of his childhood and the occupants of Billingsgate Street, Greenwich. 'George Barnes lived at No.13. He was, in his younger days, a seaman but now sold bundles of firewood and coal which he used to dredge from the Thames, going out in his rowing boat to collect any that may have fallen into the river from the coal barges as they were unloading at the wharfside. The catsmeat man, George Stubbs, lived at No. 17. He made his living doing door-to-door calls selling horsemeat wrapped in newspaper. Joseph Cridland was a cobbler. He worked in the front room of No. 35. A little bespectacled man and a craftsman at his job. The smell of leather, bees-wax and tallow, and the sound of his hammer on a small anvil together with the whirl of his buffing lathe was his trademark.' Mrs V. Small was born in Pelton Road, East Greenwich in 1926. As a child she collected lumps of chalk from the river's edge to whiten her Woolworth's shoes, bought at 6d each, then 'collected all old driftwood for Mum to burn in the copper Monday morning for the washing.'

Deptford Market in the High Street has long been a popular shopping and meeting place. Some stallholders have several generations of market trading behind them.

In 1742 George II's admiralty decided they needed a bigger and better ships' victualling stores, moved to Deptford and built the Royal Victualling Yard, later named after Queen Victoria. After a succession of fires destroyed most of the Yard the present naval-style buildings were erected. Formerly the rum stores, with which the navy was very generous in those days, they have now been modernised into apartments. The Stairs were purpose built for landing victuals and are still in good order.

J.P. Palmer Ltd's Paynes Paper wharf, Deptford has a graceful river frontage beside Watergate Stairs. Once a thriving industry, the wharf has lain idle for many years awaiting a decision on its future.

Near Deptford Creek was Deptford power station. Colliers and barges continuously supplied vast quantities of coal here until the power stations were de-commissioned. Upriver from the power station is the massive Borthwick's wharf which could cold store up to 300,000 carcases of beef and lamb, while downstream are sited the wharves of the General Steam Navigation Co Ltd, long gone by 1976.

A Sun tug approaching foreign cargo ships moored at Convoys and Palmer's wharves at Greenwich.

The Greenwich Night Pageant, in aid of naval and Greenwich charities, was probably one of the first son et lumiére extravaganzas, taking place as it did 'between the Wren buildings of the Royal Naval College' from 16-24 June, 1934, 'Sunday excepted', with 2,500 performers, the full band of the First (Chatham) Division of HM Royal Marines while the South Metropolitan Electric Light & Power Co. Ltd, 183 High Street, Lewisham, provided electric colour floodlighting at $\frac{1}{2}$d per unit.

SUPPLY OF SPIRITS, Etc., TO H.M. SHIPS.

To comply with H.M. Customs' Regulations, *it is necessary that Form No. 64 should be filled in* and presented as an order. This Form can be obtained from the Society on application.

No. SPIRITS. (From Bond.)	Per doz.	Per octave 14 gallons cased.	Per qtr. cask 28 gallons cased.	No.	Per doz.	Per octave 14 gallons cased.	Per qtr. cask 28 gallons cased.
WHISKY (SCOTCH).				**GIN.**			
4 Special Blend, Pot Still, Very Fine Pure Malt, 9 years old, Society's Blend (Mark IV.), 18 u.p.	58/-	£18 4	£35 13	1 Unsweetened, 17 u.p.	30/-	£7	£13 16
				3 Plymouth (Coates & Co.)	38/-		
1 Fine Old Blended Scotch Whisky. (A blend of Old Vatted Highland Malt and Old Grain Whiskies) 18 u.p.	45/	£13 13	£26 10	**BRANDY.**			
				1 Pale Cognac	56/-		
				3 Pale Choice Old Cognac	68/-		
WHISKY (IRISH).				7 Very Fine Liqueur Cognac	92/-		
J. Jameson & Son's *** Pot Still, 25 u.p.	62/-			J. & F. Martell's ***	78/-		
RUM.				J. Hennessy's ***	78/-		
1 Old Jamaica, 22 u.p.	45/-			All Proprietary Brandies and Whiskies quoted are sold as described by the various Shippers and as received from them.			

ALL PRICES ARE SUBJECT TO MARKET FLUCTUATIONS.

According to this 1934 wine list it was possible to purchase a case of one dozen bottles of Moët et Chandon champagne for 87/- : £4.35 today, or a dozen bottles of Old Tawny port for a mere 50/- (£2.50) duty free. But before going green with envy, remember a docker's wages only came to about 12/- (60p) per day (£3.60 per week.) With rent at 5/- (25p) a week and a large family to feed and clothe a man was lucky to have enough for his daily pint of wallop, never mind anything fancy.

The winners of the Novice Race at Greenwich Regatta in August 1948. Len Coker, waterman, is second stroke, third oarsman from the stern.

The Mitre public house won the 'Publican's Fours' race at Greenwich in 1959, as Len Coker is pleased to remember. He is wearing the second fancy hat on the left as the crew pose in front of their boat shed.

'Jolly Wally' alias Johnny D. Scott was born in Sheerness in 1928 and lived in Chatham for his childhood. He has been busking for over thirty years, ten of them at Greenwich near the *Cutty Sark* and was a children's entertainer until Christmas 1986. Jolly Wally makes his own Band Wagons and at present has two. He has worked by invitation in Europe, America, Japan and Malta. He gave a Royal Command Performance at Victoria Palace in 1984, another at the children's RCP in 1988 and was in the Guiness Book of Records for playing seven hours non stop. He is proud to have three children and three grandchildren.

In 1973 docker Len Coker was handed his severance pay by Gee Stevedoring and found himself unemployed after thirty-seven years. In his time he had worked for well-known firms such as Pope and Bond. With his money he and Frank Driver bought *Dogwood Fisher*, a barge, fitting it out as a floating garage supplying diesel, petrol etc, chandlery and engineering services to boats. The barge carried 2,000 gallons of petrol. Some of their more well-known boating customers were Paul and Linda McCartney and Denny Laine, and John Malcolm who acted in the film *Enemy at the Door* as the Nazi, Otto Kluge.

Pope & Bond's bargeyard entrance, established
in 1770. In 1966 Bill Pope and Ben Bond took
over, repairing barges, tugs and motor vessels for
lighterage firms. With 5,000 lightermen in the
1950s, each with a barge, there was plenty to do.
Contract work later dwindled to Cleanaways' 41
purpose-built barges used to convey London's
300,000 tons of annual waste from
Westminster's Grosvenor Dock, now closed.
The barges were covered by McGregor's
hatching, pulled across the 20ft x 86ft opening
on nylon wheels by rotating drum. Pope and
Bond renovated the capstan, bowsprit and
figurehead of *Cutty Sark*. Both men served seven
year apprenticeships. Bill worked on wood, iron
and steel barges, tugs and motor vessels and
caulked, rivetted and built for the Thames Dry
Dock & Engineering Co. Ben started out in
insurance before working at W. & N. Sparks,
Limehouse on spritzel sailing barges. In the war
he coverted dumb barges into invasion tank
landing craft to convince the Germans of a
forthcoming invasion. Barges, at 500 tons, were
used to anchor barrage balloons along the river.
With the decline in barge work the yard closed,
in August 1996, but hopes to re-open as a
working museum.

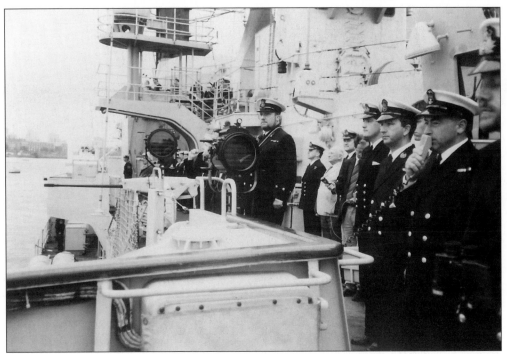

When ships of the Royal Navy pass the Royal Naval College the crew are on parade. Having sounded the bosun's call, officers and crew of HMS *Gloucester* stand to attention until piped down.

A tethering of tugs at Greenwich Pier flanked by the Royal Naval College and clipper ship, *Cutty Sark*. She was docked at Greenwich for the 1951 Festival of Britain; her permanent berth from 1954. Ben Dillon remembers sitting on Garden Stairs watching 14,000 ton Cunarders turning in the Reach. 'They had to be towed stern first by two Alexander Sun tugs, then headed in. What a sight that was. My friend Wally Cook's dad bought him a rowboat to earn his living and many a day I helped him row a ship's crew out to Greenwich Buoys at a shilling a time.'

The remains of a substantial jetty could still be seen in front of the Royal Naval College in 1978 but these were regarded as river hazards so were removed.

Trafalgar Tavern and Then Ship came into their own, April to September, renowned for their in-season whitebait dinners. Nineteenth century locals soon found themselves competing with visitors for a table to dine. Curlew Rowing Club HQ is at The Trafalgar. Nearby, Alpha Towage provide lighterage services and The Yacht is still a popular pub for young watermen.

The paddle steamer *Elizabethan* is a well-known sight on the Thames. Here, she sails down from the Upper Pool to Greenwich with passengers eager to watch a barge race, ready to follow the competitors back up to Blackfriars Bridge.

An entrant in the 1980 Tall Ships Race with her crew, dressed over all, on the yards of their three-masted ship.

The Queen was officially 60 years of age in April, 1986. A grand children's parade was organised. Children from around Greenwich sailed up the Thames in chartered boats. Alderwood's was the *Viscountess*; just the right size for us. Landing at Westminster, we walked with our 'Happy Birthday' banners to St James's Palace. We came from schools across London. Everyone held a bunch of daffodils. The mounted police were smiling as they escorted us up the Mall accompanied by brass bands. We were all allowed through the Palace gates into the Yard to see the Queen and Prince Philip on the balcony. It was a great day. Pity it rained!

Lovell's extensive wharves, below Greenwich power station, were still in use until recently.

Six
Captain Grinsted and the *Princess Alice*

A greatest disaster and tragedy on the Thames was the sinking of the London Steamship Company's pleasure paddle steamer Princess Alice *in which 600 men, women and children drowned within yards of safety. On Tuesday, 3 September, 1878 the* Princess Alice *sailed on a day trip to Gravesend and Sheerness returning to London early that evening. In command was highly experienced Captain William Grinsted. Among the many passengers were Mrs Eugenie Hawks, owner of the Anchor and Hope pub at Charlton, a group of 'ladies of the night' from the Seven Dials district of London, forty indigent ladies from Smithfield's Cowcross Mission, a group from a Bible class and several people in wheelchairs. As the steamer rounded the bend between Crossness and Margaret Ness near Tripcock Point, she met the steam collier,* Bywell Castle *which had just off-loaded her cargo at Millwall Dock and was returning off the south shore under Captain Tom Harrison to Newcastle. What happened next is still open to speculation as, despite two official enquiries, there was disagreement as to how such a terrible accident could occur when both Captain Grinsted, with 20 years worth of expertise, and Captain Harrison with 37 years' experience, were Master Mariners with justifiable reputations for meticulously safe sailing. Yet at 20.45 the 370 gross tons* Bywell Castle *ploughed into the 250 gross tons* Princess Alice *which split amidships, stern and bows folding upwards, and sank within minutes drowning all but a few fortunate survivors. Victorian ladies, lacking opportunities to learn swimming and in voluminous, waterlogged dresses had little chance to reach shore which was only 300 yards away. Many died choking on pollution from the Southern outfall works as the ebb tide swept them towards Erith. Some bodies were not recovered for several days. Those brought ashore were mainly taken to Woolwich Dockyard and Roff's Wharf, numbered if names were not known, then laid out for relatives to claim. Mike Cooley says some bodies drifted as far as Gravesend where they were laid for claiming in the pier waiting room. There are three monuments to the disaster: at Crossness near the scene of the accident; a brass plaque dedicated to one of the victims is in St Mary Magdalene church, Woolwich. A large marble celtic cross at Woolwich cemetery marks the grave of unclaimed victims and was paid for by public subscription when 23,000 contributors from all over Britain each gave 6d (2½p).*

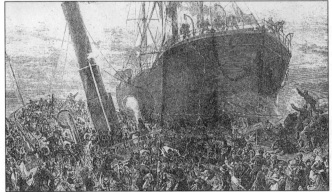

The end of a happy day's outing at Gravesend as the collier, *Bywell Castle*, runs down the pleasure paddle cruiser *Princess Alice* at a time when many passengers were below decks enjoying refreshments as they cruised home in happy mood.

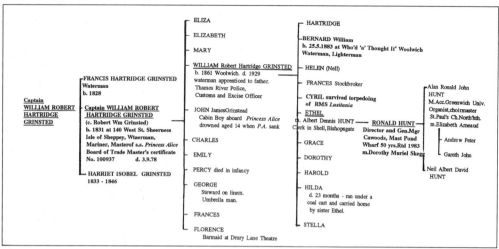

The Grinsted family tree, tracing the line directly from Captain Grinsted's father through to his great-great-grandchildren.

The family tree contains the following information:

Captain WILLIAM ROBERT HARTRIDGE GRINSTED

- **FRANCIS HARTRIDGE GRINSTED** Waterman b. 1828
- **Captain WILLIAM ROBERT HARTRIDGE GRINSTED** (c. Robert Wm Grinsted) b. 1831 at 140 West St. Sheerness Isle of Sheppey, Wtaerman, Masterof s.s. *Princess Alice* Board of Trade Master's certificate No. 100937 d. 3.9.78
- **HARRIET ISOBEL GRINSTED** 1833 - 1846

Children of Francis Hartridge Grinsted:

- ELIZA
- ELIZABETH
- MARY
- WILLIAM Robert Hartridge GRINSTED b. 1861 Woolwich. d. 1929 waterman apprenticed to father. Thames River Police, Customs and Excise Officer
  - HARTRIDGE
  - BERNARD William b. 25.5.1883 at "Who'd 'a' Thought It" Woolwich Waterman, Lighterman
  - HELEN (Nell)
  - FRANCES Stockbroker
  - CYRIL survived torpedoing of RMS *Lusitania*
  - ETHEL m. Albert Dennis HUNT ——— RONALD HUNT Clerk in Shell, Bishopsgate Director and Gen.Mgr Cawoods, Mast Pond Wharf 50 yrs.Rtd 1983 m.Dorothy Muriel Skegg
    - Alan Ronald John HUNT M.Acc.Greenwich Univ. Organist,choirmaster St.Paul's Ch.North'hth. m.Elizabeth Ameaud
      - Andrew Peter
      - Gareth John
    - Neil Albert David HUNT
  - GRACE
  - DOROTHY
  - HAROLD
  - HILDA d. 23 months - ran under a coal cart and carried home by sister Ethel.
  - STELLA
- JOHN JamesGrinstead Cabin Boy aboard *Princess Alice* drowned aged 14 when *P.A.* sank
- CHARLES
- EMILY
- PERCY died in infancy
- GEORGE Steward on liners. Umbrella man.
- FRANCES
- FLORENCE Barmaid at Drury Lane Theatre

Albert Dennis Hunt, born 1869, grandson of Captain Grinsted (not shown on family tree). Albert's watch chain (called 'Alberts', after the Consort's own) is reverse-looped in the fashion of the day. The starched, stand-up collar must have been uncomfortable to wear while playing as a violinist's neck needs to be flexible.

The Grinsted family 24 years after the disaster. Captain Grinsted's grandchildren, Bernard, aged 19, in a smart panama hat, Ethel (12), Cyril (14), Frank (16) and Helen, 'Nell' (18) stand at the back behind their parents, Emma Harriet Grinsted (44) holding baby Stella (1) and PC William Robert Hartridge Grinsted (41). Blanche (11) sits on the floor beside mother, while Grace (10), sits beside their father. The Jack of the ill-fated *Princess Alice* hangs over the window, reminding William of his father and 14-year-old brother, John James Grinsted, a cabin boy aboard the *Princess* who both drowned.

There appears to be no existing photograph of Captain Grinsted, but a sketch gives some idea of his appearance.

No.	When and Where Died	Name and Surname	Sex	Age	Rank or Profession	Cause of Death	Signature, Description, and Residence of Informant	When Registered	Signature of Registrar
141	3rd September 1878 Gallions Reach River Thames	Sarah King (the ebb A)	Female	30 years	a Widow	Drowning from the "Princess Alice" Steamer	Certificate received from Chas J. Carttar Coroner for Kent Inquest held 4th September 1878 to 27th November 1878	Sixth December 1878	J. Tufnell Registrar
142	3rd September 1878 Gallions Reach River Thames	William Isaac Cambert	Male	35 years	Music Publisher	Drowning owing to a collision between the Bywell Castle Barnes and the Princess Alice Steamer whereby the Princess Alice Steamer was Sunk	Certificate received from Chas J. Carttar Coroner for Kent Inquest held 4th September 1878 to 27th November 1878	Sixth December 1878	J. Tufnell Registrar
143	3rd September 1878 Gallions Reach River Thames	Samuel Lowry	Male	56 years	Gentleman	Drowning from the "Princess Alice" Steamer	Certificate received from Chas J. Carttar Coroner for Kent Inquest held 4th September 1878 to 27th November 1878	Sixth December 1878	J. Tufnell Registrar
144	3rd September 1878 Gallions Reach River Thames	a Susannah Law	Female	52 years	Spinster	Drowning from the "Princess Alice" Steamer	Certificate received from Chas J. Carttar Coroner for Kent Inquest held 4th September 1878 to 27th November 1878	Sixth December 1878	J. Tufnell Registrar
145			Male	15		Drowning from the "Princess Alice" Steamer	Certificate received from Chas J. Carttar Coroner for Kent Inquest held 4th September 1878	Sixth	J. Tufnell

The Registrar of Deaths at Woolwich Arsenal had more work than he could reasonably cope with once victims were identified and reported. His entries filled many pages and his 'clerkly hand' suffered as a consequence. The date of every person drowned had to be recorded. It took over a month to carry out all the inquests. GLHL

In Memory of
NEARLY
SEVEN HUNDRED PASSENGERS,
Who perished by the sinking of the
Saloon Steamer,
"PRINCESS ALICE,"
IN THE THAMES, OFF WOOLWICH,
September 3rd, 1878.

The tragedy touched the nation, especially when the real Princess Alice, after whom the steamer was named, died three months later. This is just one of several memorial cards issued at 6d. each to benefit the families of victims and to pay for a gravestone for the unnamed. In an era when death called for black edged writing paper and even piano legs were draped for decency's sake, pious widows often wore black for the rest of their lives to show devotion to their late husbands.

The flag of the *Princess Alice* is at Wapping Police Museum. PC Keith Gotch recounts a heroic yarn of the fatal day: A Thames Division policeman was aboard the *Princess* as a passenger. He bravely reached his drowning wife and got her ashore, rescuing the flag as the ship went down, only to find that the lady he had saved was a stranger and his poor wife drowned. Happily, because of their shared ordeal, the policeman and the rescued lady eventually fell in love and were married. MPTD

No.	When Died	Name	Sex	Age	Rank	Cause of Death	Signature of Informant	When Regd.	Signature of Registrar
52	3rd September 1878 Galleon's Reach River Thames	William Robert Hartridge Grinstead	Male	46 years	Captain "Princess Alice"	Drowning from the "Princess Alice" Steamer	Certificate received from Chas. J. Carttar Coroner for Kent. Inquest held 4th September 1878 & 27th November 1878	Sixth December 1878	J. Tuffield Registrar

1878. DEATHS in the District of Woolwich Arsenal in the County of Kent

The captain's family name 'Grinsted', usually inaccurately spelt as 'Grinstead' in newspaper articles, is wrongly written on Captain Grinsted's death certificate so it is easy to see where the error arose. Deptford honoured Captain Grinsted by naming a road off Evelyn Street after him: unfortunately, they too have misspelled it. GLHL

Not far from Woolwich cemetery's chapel of rest stands a large, ornate celtic style white marble cross. Around its plinth is carved a memorial to the victims buried in this mass grave for 160 bodies left unclaimed after their death, waiting as long as decency allowed before being interred. No names appear there, for none were known.

The double wedding of two of the Grinsted sisters was quite a fashionable affair as can be seen by the stylish outfits worn by the company – and look at that row of beautifully polished shoes!

TO THE GLORY OF GOD
AND IN LOVING MEMORY OF FREDERICK WHOMES
WHO WITH FIVE HUNDRED AND NINETY OTHERS PERISHED
NEAR THIS PLACE IN THAT AWFUL CALAMITY THE
SINKING OF THE "PRINCESS ALICE" 3RD SEPTEMBER 1878

"JESUS SAITH UNTO HER THY BROTHER SHALL RISE AGAIN"

Over 200 years old, St Mary Magdalene church is on a site older than Domesday, says Donald Hunt, lay administrator. A memorial plaque to Frederick Whomes, one of the *Alice*'s victims, is kept in shining order by Mrs Enid Webb who has a newspaper cutting commemorating the catastrophe. The first inquest, held by Coroner C.J. Cartter of Blackheath, heard the Board of Trade licensed the ship, new in 1865, to carry 486 passengers but increased this to 936 in 1878 after a refit. The BoT passed the ship's one lifeboat and a longboat as adequate safety precautions although these held 60 people at most. Estelle Routledge's grandmother, Anne Collard (25) in service to a Court dressmaker, survived. Lynne Andrews of Gillingham lost her great-grandmother with three of her children. Mrs R. Hall in Devon has a box made from the wood of the wreck. The *Kentish Mercury* printed a list of the known dead on 21 September 1878.

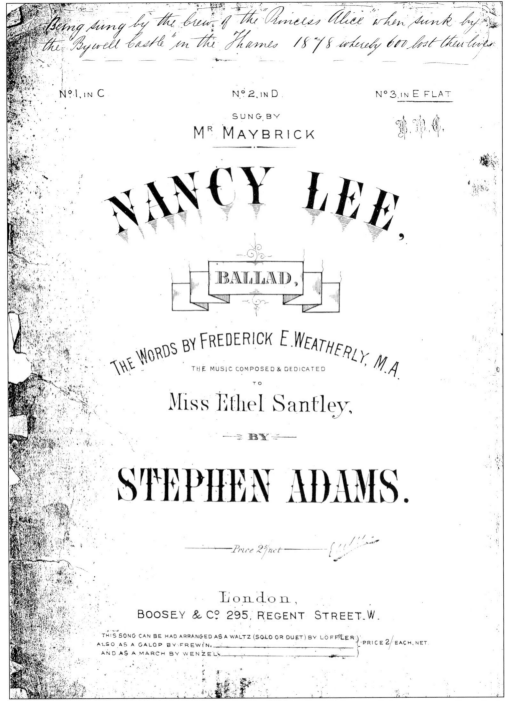

The *Princess* had a bar and restaurant on board and a live band. Some of the crew acted as choir and were singing *Nancy Lee*, a ballad, when the ship was struck. Verse three held particular pathos for those aboard: 'The bos'n pipes the watch below, Yeo ho! lads! ho!... Then here's a health afore we go... A long, long life to my sweet wife an' mates at sea; An keep our bones from Davy Jones, where'er we be...'. GLHL

Seven
Woolwich and Charlton

Harry Skelton worked on the river under his father from the age of twelve. He learned not to wear rings so there was nothing to catch or break fingers and never to keep hands in pockets: 'if you fall in the water your pockets get wet and you can't get your hands free.' Most safety lessons were learned from necessity. Having qualified as a waterman, Harry drove Rhino barges at Woolwich Arsenal docks during the Second World War. These had 2 x 500hp engines which were the origination of the outboard motor. The propellors could turn 90 degrees to give thrust in the required direction which made for accurate steering, even when carrying heavy tanks or other army transport. The Rhinos also transported petrol supplies and arms. They were each armed with a battery of Bofors guns. Mrs June Darby's grandfather, William Hayley, lost a leg in the First World War but managed to find work making tea for the men on the barges in the Mill Pond Bridge area. 'Sadly, one night he slipped on the planks that joined the barges with each other or the shore and no-one heard his cries. They found him days later, having been caught by his scarf around the propellor and rudder underneath the barge. He had thirteen children and the story was told to me by my mother years ago.' William's wife used to take in sailors as lodgers and her cousin remembers two with string tied round their trouser legs and with stuffed parrots in cages.

St Mary Magdalene church, Woolwich stands behind the remains of Cawood's Mast Pond wharf. Ronald Hunt, great-grandson of Captain Grinsted, joined Cawoods here as a junior clerk in August 1933. Cawoods transported road materials by barge along the Thames.

In 1933 it was decided there was no longer any need for the tall Woolwich B.C. Dust Destructor chimney at Mast Pond Wharf so arrangements were made with Eserin & Sons, steeplejacks, for its demolition. Unfortunately this went wrong. The chimney collapsed in a different direction to the one planned, falling across a barge moored nearby, filling it with rubble and causing a lot of costly damage. In the background can be seen barges on the tiers: that is, moored between two buoys.

The Harbour Master's house and Cutty Sark pub beside Union Wharf at Woolwich in 1988. At one time Peter Sargent and family lived here.

Ronald Hunt's uncle, Bernard, was born at the 'Who'd 'a' Thought It' beer house, 33, Woolwich High Street, owned by his maternal great-grandmother, Elizabeth Riches in 1871. Later it was merged with No. 32 and renamed the Crown and Anchor. In 1988-89 it was demolished to make way for the new Greenwich LBC Leisure Centre. Next door at the time was Hawkes Dining Rooms, favoured by waterman and employees of nearby Cawoods for their great breakfasts. Ronald Hunt and brother Doug lunched here each day after leaving home to work at Mast Pond. At that time they had not known their parents once lived next door. Pete and Leslie Sargent also ate here when Leslie worked the river. Later Hawkes became the Dragon City restaurant. At No. 35 was H. & L. Blackman, newsagents, next to Bell Water Gate Steps down to the river.

On the other side of Bell Water Gate was the Crown and Cushion, 37, Woolwich High Street. River men were well served when they landed here, with a dining room on one side and a public house on the other. The Crown and Cushion is still there, although the old Woolwich power station, just visible, has gone. Bell Water Gate is a public access slipway. At one time the Council wanted to demolish it, but a local outcry changed their minds so it is still open to the public.

In 1933 the coal yard at Mast Pond Wharf owned a steam crane which ran on rails. It was driven by a coal-fired steam boiler and the heavy fly wheel which could take a man's hand off in a second if he was careless. It was used to load coal onto barges waiting below on the river. The ice well building left of the picture was concrete lined and about 12' x 20' x 20'. After the wharf was sold to a coal merchants it took several months to fully defrost the surrounding ground .

MV *Cawarstone* transporting three senior staff of Cawoods down the Thames in 1955. They are Mr J.T. Stratford of J.T. Stratford & Sons Ltd, Woolwich motor barge builders; Ronald A. Hunt, Director of Cawood's Road Materials Ltd and charterers of MV *Cawarstone*; Harry Wilders, Manager of the lighterage department of Cawoods Road Materials Ltd.

Cawoods site, Mast Pond and remains of a concrete mulberry harbour. Ronald Hunt knows the Wharf well having started there as a young clerk, working his way up to Director and General Manager of several of Cawood's branches across the U.K. Mast Pond Wharf was originally owned by United Carlo-Gatti, Stephenson & Slater. Cawood's sold it to Redlands.

Every so often, as in 1928 and 1953, the sea musters its forces and sweeps up the Thames to flood London, flooding the land around Erith, Plumstead, Thamesmead and Woolwich. The Thames Barrier was built to control this. Begun in 1974 it was completed in October 1982. Royal Bargeman Maurice Lyne took HM The Queen and Prince Philip down in the *Royal Nore* to officially open the Barrier on 8 May 1984. The first time it was used was February 1983: tides rose exceptionally high, threatening London and the Lower Thames area. Swelling tides in 1973 washed down the east coast and across the Thames estuary, damaging both banks of the river, especially at Erith and Woolwich, completely flooding Mast Pond Wharf. Clinker from the Metropolitan Gas Works was used to raise the riverbank to 15ft at Erith.

The Thames Barrier at high water. The distinctive shell piers house hydraulic cylinders which link rocking beams to the rotating gates to raise them when there is danger of flooding.

Periodically the Thames Barrier is closed to test that its machinery is in full working order

Down river from the Barrier is the Sargent family's Unity Pier and jetty. Small boats are lifted out of the water into the barge which serves as a floating dock. The Russian submarine was part of the Baltic Fleet, brought here from Riga, Latvia under the command of Captain Vitalij Burda. U-475 is 92 metres long, can make 16.8 knots and needs a crew of 75 including officers and commisar. She can stay under water for four days at a time.

Who would expect to see a Russian submarine in the Thames. Its sleek outline arousing memories for ex-RN sailors. Mark Sturton's Foxtrot U-475, one of the larger class vessels, is presently moored near the Thames Barrier. Painted original black, she is quite hard to spot when sailing past unless, of course, you happen to know she is there. She is surprisingly roomy inside. The original battery storage area is big enough for a party, but the crew must have been horizontally challenged: anyone over 5ft would be hanging over their bunk ends. U-475 may go to Bristol in 1997.

Paramount's *Indiana Jones and the Temple of Doom* conjures up visions of high adventure and danger. The steam cable layer, *John W. McKay* was used to transport the hero to exotic places. Before that, she sailed down the Thames through the Barrier to Tilbury to be fitted for her new role.

Will Crooks paddle ferry crossing to North Woolwich at ebb tide. Gus Baulch recalls other ferries were *Squires*, *Gordon* and *John Benn*. The Woolwich Ferry was always free. In October 1873 the ferry was stopped due to thick fog. Determined to get over to work at Beckton Gas Works and Henley's telegraph factory, 11 men and boys paid 2d each for a waterman to take them across. The boat, lost in the fog, ran under *Princess Alice's* stern moored in her usual spot off Woolwich. Despite frantic efforts to fend off the boat they were drawn by the tide and sucked under the steamer, drowning all aboard. A local subscription raised £777 for the bereaved families. The tragedy led to the building of the Woolwich foot tunnel. PLA

At one time the Arsenal was a sensitive area, with guards on the gates and a high wall all round to keep out anyone who was too curious. Much of the grounds have now been sold off (Henry VIII would have had trouble keeping a level head if he'd known they were to be axed) and a new housing development sits where armaments were once kept. Workshops still flank the river but they stand empty; no longer are bullets packed into trays or guns assembled there for the army's use.

Machine shops for munitions were an essential part of the Arsenal. Guns have been made here since Henry VIII's time and during the Second World Waw many Woolwich ladies still remember manufacturing, assembling and packing armaments ready for shipping to our troops abroad.

During both world wars the jetties were used to embark tanks, Scammell lorries, other heavy transport and troops from nearby Royal Artillery barracks. John Hibbert recalls that after the war the Ministry of Transport sold or bare-boat chartered all the American purpose-built, mass produced British Liberty vessels to shipping companies as there was a surplus. Before use they were 'strapped', otherwise they were inclined to break in half 'like carrots'. At 10,000 tons they were a handy size and had a life of 10 years.

On Charlton's river bank are several wartime pill boxes, built in case the Germans ever managed to get this far up the Thames. Constructed without benefit of damp courses they suffered from condensation and were uncomfortable posts for sentries at the best of times. The original river wall was built in mediaeval times and stretched from the Isle of Grain to Greenwich.

In 1821 Tom Cribb was awarded the title, 'Champion for Life' as England's finest boxer. Tom, aged 13, came to London to seek his fortune, working as apprentice bell hanger before becoming a wharf porter and sailor. In 1805 he won his first of many bare-fisted fights, only ever losing one. In 1821 he was a bodyguard at George IVs coronation. His winnings bought a London pub but he lost all his money and returned to live with his son, a Woolwich baker. He died in 1848. Three years later a lion monument was erected in lonely splendour to his memory in St Mary Magdalene's churchyard, Woolwich.

Eight

Sargents on the Thames

Some family names – Livett, Harris, Fagan, Pudney, Rickwood, Montague, Phelps, Skelton and many others are threaded through Thames history. The Sargents go back over 300 years. Great-great-grandfather Thomas Sargent was an eigtheenth-century Woolwich Dockyard shipwright. Valerie traced their family back to 1793 but their river connection were earlier, trades being handed down from father to son. Joseph, youngest of Thomas's six children, married Sarah, daughter of a Waterman engineer. They had eight children. His fourth child, Joseph had twelve children, ten of them boys, all becoming Watermen and Freemen of the River. In 1878 Thomas's son, Joseph (40) and wife were expecting their sixth child, William. Joseph was looking for a larger family house. On 3 September the Princess Alice sank in the Thames. Among the drowned was Mrs Eugenie Hawkes, licensee of the riverside Anchor and Hope public house, Charlton, which came up for sale soon after.This was ideal for his expanding family and offered the opportunity to retire as a waterman while keeping contact with river friends during their time off. The Anchor and Hope remained in the family for 99 years. Three weeks into the First World War the Corinthian and Oriole collided opposite the pub. The Oriole listed and sank. Young Joe Sargent rescued sixteen people in his skiff watched by a large crowd which afterwards slaked their thirst at the Anchor, served by licensee Louisa. In the 1918 Joseph died of respiratory complications not helped by London smog. The Anchor was base for his watermen sons, vying with each other for work, even ensuring employment by rowing to Gravesend then arranging to be towed by a ship which may later require piloting. Fraternal competition was fierce but work was plentiful when Second World War convoys required pilots. Some brothers enlisted, making more work for those left behind. The Sargents mainly relied on the collier trade, shipping coal from the north east to Thames power stations and home consumption. Often all the brothers were underway in separate ships from the same port to different jetties. By 1951 rivalry finally ceased when they formed Sargent Bros (Thames) Ltd, purchasing Unity, an old Thames sailing barge, moored at Charlton exactly on the site of the present Thames Barrier: one hold was used as an office, the other as boat repair workshop. Unity was replaced by a permanent jetty later commandeered for the Barrier site. After much legal wrangling the GLC agreed to provide a purpose-built office, workshop and pier 300m downstream. The River changed; colliers became redundant, several brothers retired and the work flagged. Leslie's son, Peter, suggested building a disco pleasure boat. The idea was a huge success. Built in 1977, the Enchanté also did round-the-barrier cruises until the 1989 Marchioness disaster. Valerie, John and Peter now run the company. For a while Peter lived by the pier in a modular houseboat. David, sixth generation on the River, is apprenticed to his father Peter, continuing in the family business.

The Sargent family in the 1950s with Grandma Sargent second from the left.

Having earned their Freedom of the river it was natural for the Sargent men to go in the navy during the war. Two of the brothers attended Royal Naval Gunnery School at Whale Island. Leslie, Pete's father, is near the front and his brother Bobby is second row from the top.

When Pete's Uncle Bob got married to Auntie Marge, naturally the reception was held at the family's Anchor and Hope in Charlton. Grandma Sargent had all her grown children around her and it was a real family wedding. Only son Ronnie was missing, presumed at work. Harry is at the left, then Joe, Rosie (who married a Cory's tug skipper and moved to Cornwall), Tommy (Dolly's second husband), Archie, John (Val's father), Bob, Grandma Sargent, Bill, Wally (a half brother), and Les (Pete's Dad).

Vasey's Wharf, from the Anchor and Hope, was kept busy importing bricks and building materials in the 1940s. Three small children play on the end of the causeway where Great-Grandfather Sargent brought his belongings by barge in 1878 when he first took it over the pub from the previous owner, Mrs Hawkes, who died aboard *Princess Alice*. Joseph dragged all his goods and chattels up the steep causeway to the Anchor and Hope at the top without help.

To keep track of their work, watermen maintain a daily log. Leslie Sargent's workbook meticulously records the date; whether a vessel was to be moored, unmoored, removed or towed; each vessel's name; where it was to be met and left, at a jetty, buoy, wharf or dock and whether requiring day or night attendance. On 22 June 1942 he recorded in keeping with his daily record a berth of another kind: 'Em gave birth to a Baby Son' – Baby Son with capital letters in the same way he would have recorded the name of a ship. The child was Peter Sargent.

Bobby Sargent became Master of the Company of Watermen and Lightermen from 1971 to 1972 and was the proud wearer of this Jewel. The wording reads: '1514. AT COMMANDE OF OUR SVPERIOVHS' (At command of our superiors) being the date the Company was founded and motto.

Harry Sargent, Waterman, was Dolly's first husband.

his Indenture Witnesseth, That _Joseph Jarvis_
Carden Son of _Joseph Carden_
of the Parish of _Thartford_
in the _County of Kent_ doth put himse
Apprentice to _Joseph Carden_ of said
of the Parish of _foresaid_
in the C_____ _foresaid_ a Freema

1514—1859

of the Company of Watermen and Lightermen of the River Thames,

to learn his Art, and with him (after the manner of an Apprentice) to dwell and serve upon the River of Thames from the Day of the Date hereof until the full End and Term of   years from thence next following, to be fully complete and ended; during which Term the said Apprentice his said Master faithfully shall serve as aforesaid, his Secrets keep, his lawful Commandments every where gladly do; He shall do no damage to his said Master, nor see it to be done by others, but that he to his Power, shall let or forthwith give Warning to his said Master of the same; He shall not waste the Goods of his said Master, nor lend them unlawfully to any; He shall not commit Fornication, nor contract Matrimony within the said Term; He shall not play at Cards, Dice, Tables, nor any other unlawful games whereby his said Master may have any Loss with his own Goods, or others, during the said Term, without License of his said Master he shall not buy nor sell; He shall not haunt Taverns, nor Play-Houses, nor absent himself from his Master's Service Day nor Night, unlawfully, but in all things as a faithful Apprentice he shall behave himself towards his said Master, and all his, during the said Term. And the said Master in consideration of the

the said Apprentice in the same Art which he useth by the best means that he can, shall teach, and instruct, or cause to be taught and instructed, finding unto the said Apprentice Meat, Drink, Apparel, Lodging and all other Necessaries according to the Custom of the City of London. And for the true Performance of all and every the said Covenants and Agreements, each of the said Parties bind themselves unto the other by these Presents. IN WITNESS whereof the Parties above-named in these Indentures interchangeably have put their Hands and Seals.—

Dated _twelfth_   Day of _June_   **18**

Signed and Delivered, at Watermen's Hall, London, in the Presence of

Joseph W. Sargent

Members of the Court.   _Joseph Sargent_

_____ Clerk.

N.B.—The Indentures must bear date the day they are executed; and if any Money is given or contracted for with the Master and Apprentice, the same must be inserted in Words at full length in the body of the Indentures, and the Duty thereon paid by the Master to the Stamp Office, in London, within One Month after the execution thereof, under a penalty of Fifty Pounds, and double the amount of the Premium given, and the Indentures become void.

Great Grandfather Joseph's parchment indentures, dated 12 June 1888. At the end of his seven year apprenticeship Joe went to Waterman's Hall to be accepted into the Company of Watermen and Lightermen. Finishing his apprenticeship was an important step in a lad's life. If his master was satisfied his work passed strict tests, the ceremonially robed Barge Masters at Waterman's Hall presented the second half of the original document, specially cut when first starting his time: the two halves matched exactly. He was then a Freeman of the River. Backing the Duty Stamp is a second stamp with a crown above an entwined 'VR', Queen Victoria.

Lightermen and watermen's licences are issued annually by the Port of London Authority. The licence is acknowledgement that he is fully competent in the crafts, rules and laws of the river and can be revoked if he fails his job in any of these areas. Separate licences are issued for watermen and lightermen, but some carry both licenses as did Joe Sargent.

Father and son with the new work bench Leslie had just given Pete for his eighth birthday.

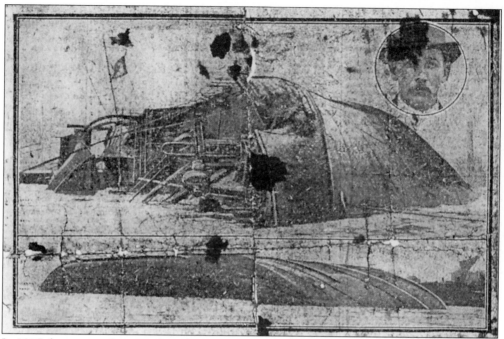

In 1915 there was a disaster when the steamship *Corinthian* rammed the smaller *Oriole*, sinking her off Charlton, not far from the Sargent's pier. There were no fatalities, but sixteen passengers' lives were saved by Joe Sargent who also salvaged the smaller ship. Having put in a claim, Joseph Sargent snr. later received a letter from his solicitors regarding the salvaging of the *Oriole*, awarding his son Joe the sum of £50 salvage money.

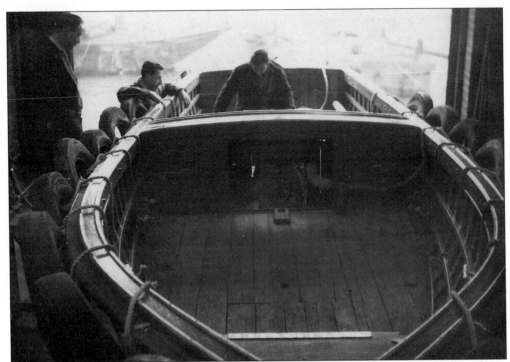

The Sargents' old pier had a boathouse before it was pulled down to make room for span 'A' of the Thames Barrier. *Endurance*, a good ash-framed motorised workboat with oak planking, was put in for a new engine a refurbishment in 1962. Johnson & Jorgenson's glass factory, since demolished, is in the background.

When it was ready to re-launch it was discovered the tide was about two feet lower than expected. As the boat was needed it had to be launched regardless, so 'out she went,' making heavy weather of it as she did so!

Left: 'It may not look like much of a home...' this is how the barge *Unity* appeared as the Sargents first saw it when it when delivered to Lovell's wharf. Right: After much emptying, cleaning, painting and a caravan had been lowered onto it, the barge was beginning to look like a real houseboat.

Left: Pete and Pat in their floating home. Right: However living on the river in the cold weather is not such fun and in winter 1970 Pat needed her furry boots to keep her warm while scraping the ice off the newly-named *Unity*.

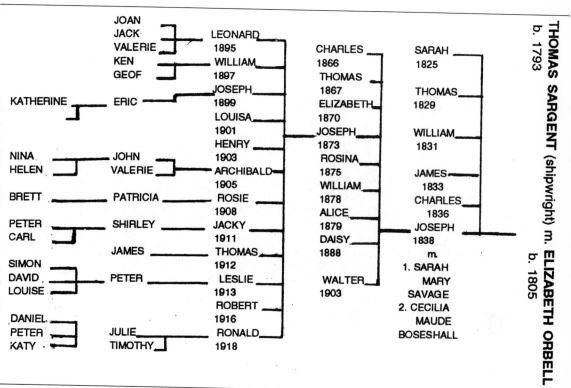

The Sargent Family Tree showing six generations of Freemen of the River.

In 1978 the Sargents bought a new boat, *Enchanté*. With Pete at the wheel and three of his uncles as crew Les, cousin John, Ron and Tom give her a trial run.

Enchanté was purpose built as a Thames pleasure boat at Conyer Creek in 1977.

After many years of good service on the river it was decided to sell *Enchanté* to Stuart Cordner in Scotland. To get her up there she had to be transported by road and this meant cutting her in half, lengthways: a feat carried out at Welbeck Wharf.

Once *Enchanté* arrived at Loch Lomond she was successfully re-assembled and is still a working boat on the picturesque lake. The present owner, Stuart, talks to Peter Sargent.

Wearing his Waterman's blazer, Tommy Sargent moored off the Anchor and Hope at Charlton in his workboat in 1973. Tommy's Uncle William was born at the Anchor and Hope a few months after the *Princess Alice* sank. Alice and Daisy were born soon after.

Through the river mists, the sixteenth-century Irish longboat *Dim Riv* glided up the Thames carrying a lone Uillean piper and his Irish chieftain Grace O'Malley; Granuaille in the Gaelic. Their destination is Greenwich where, in 1593, Grace met Elizabeth I at the palace to plead for justice for her people. In the 1987 re-enactment of Grace's courageous voyage, escorted by the Irish sail training boat, *Asgard II*, Pete Sargent was the river pilot, accompanied by his son David.

Nine

Thamesmead and Erith

Thamesmead and Erith are both the beginning and the end of our pictorial voyage. It was at Crossness, within sight of Gallions Reach the Princess Alice met her fate. Opposite the point of collision is Crossness sewage station built thirteen years before, in the grounds of the Southern Outfall Main Drainage Works. Crossness houses the world's four largest rotative beam engines, now at the end of their working life yet ready to start anew as an industrial museum. Built in 1899, in retirement they are being restored to their former splendour by a dedicated workforce. At Belvedere, between Thamesmead and Erith, the dream of pollution and noise-free vehicles which began with Queen Victoria's electric car, was revived by Sir Clive Sinclair at Cambridge and is being advanced in spectacular manner by innovative Belvedere designer Adam Harper. Thamesmead built twenty years ago, was created on former marshland where once mudlarkers delved hopefully for treasure. The Erith Sea Scouts, started in 1980, have a sailing barge for their HQ. Erith's Sea Cadets' first minesweeper T.S. Woolwich, commander Gordon Dyer, ex-RN, was moored at the Erith Police jetty but moved to its present pontoon to comply with safety regulations. Erith's deepwater pier and ballast wharves are now closed for redevelopment but in 1885 this was a pleasant residential village. The Erith YC HQ was aboard the Gypsy while the Corinthian YCHQ was ashore. Both clubs encouraged amateur yachting. Erith was a popular place from which sailing races started. The Erith YC is still going strong, with dozens of small craft moored offshore and on blocks in the club grounds. It was near here the Barons met King John's Commisioners to talk terms after the signing of Magna Carta: They were transported along the river by Royal Watermen. Henry VIII intended to build a Royal Dockyard here but shifting sandbanks made it unsuitable and Woolwich was chosen instead. A steamboat called regularly at the pier and a ferry ran between Erith and Coldharbour Point across the river. Most people travelled their hour's journey by train from London. Fares cost 3/9d First Class (18½p), 1/10d Second Class (9p) and 1/3d Third Class (6½p) …Class distinctions were made, but you also got the service you paid for. Vickers and Maxim had their engineering works at Erith, where Hiram Maxim invented the first automatic machinegun. Vickers, Son & Maxim employed 4,000 workers producing armamanets and aircraft for the Boer War. Erith Yacht Club member, Mr I.K. Holland referred to the untamed beauty of adjacent fenland which is the last refuge for much estuary wildlife in the area and their way of life is carefully monitored.

The Barge, *Unity*, in service carrying a hayload down the Thames. Later, when used as an office on the river before the jetty was built, *Unity* leaked badly. Though only afloat two hours at high tide she had a huge bung pushed into her bottom to keep afloat, which was removed to let water out. Pete Sargent was at the cinema one night when he suddenly remembered the bung… and it was nearly high water! Rushing back on his scooter he found *Unity* wallowing in 3ft of water and had to hold his breath to reach down and bang home the bung: a job he never forgot again.

Margaret Ness lighthouse at Gallions Point, Thamesmead.

Barges moored off Tripcock Point, Gallions Reach at approximately the same location the *Princess Alice* was sunk by the *Bywell Castle*.

Old jetties at Erith cast broken images on the water. Further out, looking upriver towards Thamesmead, is HMS *Soberton*. Erith Sea Cadets have owned three minesweepers. *Soberton*, moored in the roads of Erith Reach, is mahogany built with phospher bronze anti-magnetic metalwork. When older, many cadets go on to join the Navy, say John and Francis Rule. The Sea Scouts' sailing barge is further downriver.

John Draper was the publican of the Cross Keys at Erith from 1749-1751. A fire, said to have started in the Bagatelle Room, razed the pub on 10 August 1891. It was rebuilt and opened Bank Holiday Monday, 1 August 1892. Sharon Taylor and Derek McKenzie's are the present landlords of this pleasant pub overlooking the river and reputed to be one of the oldest buildings in Erith.

London's crude nineteenth century sewage system had become a danger to its citizens. The succession of cholera epidemics was hardly surprising when raw sewage emptied into the Thames close to where the City drew its drinking water. 'The situation was seriously aggravated by the newly invented flush toilets', says David Wilkinson. Something had to be done. The Metropolitan Board of Works were given £3m for improvements and Sir Joseph Bazalgette devised the revolutionary Crossness Pumping Station. Housed in ornate Victorian Gothic, the buildings were opened 1865 by the Prince of Wales.

In 1889 the four engines, Victoria, Prince Consort, Albert Edward and Alexandria were given more powerful boilers. Each sand-cast beam weighs forty-seven tons. The four fly-wheels, each made in four parts and weighing 57-seven tons helped raise 6 tons of effluent every stroke, at 10 strokes a minute. James Watt of Birmingham, built the larger beam and Corliss designed and made the valves.

A dedicated volunteer team of twenty-five spend their weekends restoring the engines to their original state.'We could do with more help' say Jackie and Reg Barter, hopefully. Carefully cleaning and painting individual Victorian embellishments is Gillian Wilkinson, whose husband Dave is also on the committee with Mike Dunmow and Mr Dawson.

In the early 1980s: Sir Clive Sinclair, distinguished inventor of world-wide repute, invented the C5: a one-person stream-lined electric vehicle of well-made design capable of travelling short distances at 15mph. He met Adam Harper, a Belvedere designer engineer who was so impressed by their potential he bought 600 C5s. By ingenious adaptation Adam and the C5 have broken the landspeed record for electric vehicles at 115.3mph and intend to go on to 150mph.

Ten

Authorities
on the River

Anyone unfamiliar with the River might be forgiven for thinking it runs itself; but those who work with her know this is not so. The tidal river, Teddington Lock to Gravesend is under the care of the Port of London Authority, instituted in 1909. The PLA runs the docks, establishes rules of the river, provides a tug service, maintains navigational aids and many other important river aspects. The Chief Harbour Master and his officers come under the PLA, they are responsible for the safety and organised navigation on the Thames, patrolling the River to ensure all vessels comply with navigation controls, instructions and collision regulations. Founded in 1555 through an Act of Parliament, the Company of Watermen and Lightermen is for all who ply their trade on the Thames having completed a recognised apprenticeship. Elizabeth I granted their coat-of-arms. They became an independent body corporate with their own seal in 1827. Waterman's Hall was established soon after. An amended 1859 Parliamentary Act extended their powers on the Thames, establishing responsibility for determining fares, boat regulations and registrations, appointing plying places and granting licences and swan-upping. From its ranks are drawn twenty-two men honoured as Watermen to HM The Queen. The first Doggett Coat and Badge race for newly qualified Watermen, founded by Thomas Doggett, the Drury Lane actor in 1715 is now organised annually by the Fishmonger's and Watermen's Companies. Trinity House HQ was based at Deptford Strond, 1512, moving near the Tower of London in 1787. Lighthouses around Britain's coastline come under their control. Since 1988 Trinity House pilots have been under the PLA but remain independent operators, negotiating their own jobs. Most gained their expertise in the Royal or Merchant Navies and usually at senior rank. The PLA provide pilots for both River Thames and coastal piloting. Wapping Police, Thames Division, fight crime along tidal Thames. Constant thieving caused the loss of up to three-quarters of ships' cargoes. In 1798 the West India Company of Merchantmen and Parliament raised £4,200 to establish London's first uniformed police force. They patrolled the river by rowing galley and sailing cutter every six hours, effectively stemming cargo theft. Delighted Merchantmen convinced Parliament that a properly established regular force could effectively control London's criminals as well. The Metropolitan Police force was established 1829 by which time the Marine Police already had stations at Wapping, Waterloo and Blackwall. The office of HM Customs and Excise derived from Anglo-Saxon kings charging excise duty on imported articles. Cromwell extended this to raise money for his army. Charles II thought this a handy way to top up the royal coffers so kept it going. Duty laws became so convoluted that by the eighteenth century they filled twelve volumes, to which the public (who needed to know) had no access. In 1787 William Pitt simplified the rules, charging one duty for each article. Smuggling was rife, large gangs operating along the south coast and lower Thames. A preventative force was put into operation ashore and afloat with thirty-three vessels. In 1816 the army, navy and coastguards joined forces with Customs and smuggling was largely brought under control. New measures established in the early 1900s are the basis of the today's system. There was need of a fire brigade in eighteenth century London when wooden ships with heavy spreads of inflammable cotton canvas sails crowded into the Pool. Shipboard fires spread quickly to nearby vessels, yet the only means of dousing a conflagration was by lowering and dipping buckets into the Thames. The Thames Fire Brigade came into its own during the Second World War when London's docks and Woolwich Arsenal were a nightly target for enemy bombers. Their powerful water cannons easily reached blazing wharves.

Maurice Lyne, Freeman since 1956, is now a Royal Waterman and Master of the *Royal Nore*, Her Majesty's state barge. He waited twenty-two years after his application before this top honour on the River became available. Incumbents are appointed by the Lord Chancellor. Maurice is the only permanent crew member. When on duty there is also a coxswain, deckhand and a marine officer. Guests range from members of the Royal family to foreign dignitaries.

HM Queen Elizabeth's Silver Jubilee was celebrated on the river by a Royal State water procession. Escorted by Thames Division police boats, *Royal Nore* sailed to Greenwich where a guard of honour awaited her at the Royal Naval College. Scarlet-uniformed Royal Bargemen attended Her Majesty. Their office was instigated in the reign of Edward II when ruffians abounded on the River. They also do duty as coachmen on Royal coaches in procession.

A gig is a lightweight rowing boat developed in 1865 as a racing boat. The *A.J.Kirk*, a new gig, was presented to the Fishmonger's Company by the Tugmen's Guild in 1958 and the naming ceremony was held on the foreshore of the Anchor and Hope public house, Charlton.

TUGMEN'S GUILD
London and Gravesend

A Ceremony for the Naming of the Gig

"A. J. KIRK"

and the

Presentation of Gig to the Fishmongers' Company

on

Sunday, 18th May, 1958 at 11.30 a.m.

Ceremony to be held on the foreshore of the riverside tavern

"THE ANCHOR AND HOPE"

Anchor and Hope Lane,

Charlton, S.E.

Conducted by H. M. BURGESS — President 1958
Assisted by his Committee of Past Presidents

The Master of Waterman's Hall attended by Doggett Coat and Badge Men christen the *A.J.Kirk*, built by V.Radley & Sons of Spring Hill, Clapton, in appropriate style at the Anchor and Hope.

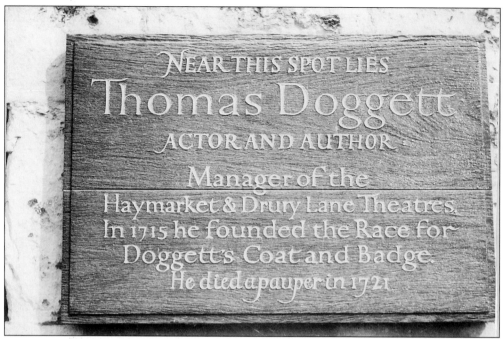

With a fanfare of trumpets the latest Doggett Coat and Badge winner is presented to the Prime Warden of the Fishmonger's Company before an assembly of past winners, resplendent in their Coats and Badges. For all his loyalty to George I and philanthropy in instituting the annual race Thomas Doggett died a pauper and lies buried in the churchyard at Eltham where a plaque commemorates his name and generous deed.

During the Second World War Frederick Dudley was a fireman at Woolwich Royal Arsenal. One night he and colleagues were up the Arsenal Tower to watch for flying bombs, keeping in telephone contact with Communications who, after a while asked, 'Anything doing ?' 'There's a flying bomb coming over from the east...now it's changed course...going north...now north-west...west, now...' 'Are you drunk ?!' came a sharp enquiry. 'No...it's going round, south...and it's back...it *must* be guided!' They had spotted one of the first guided missiles.

Frederick Dudley volunteered to do Civil Defence work during the war and was commended for his efforts. He was called up for the Air Force as a navigator although he requested transferance to flight mechanic. Instead he was put in the Fire Brigade.

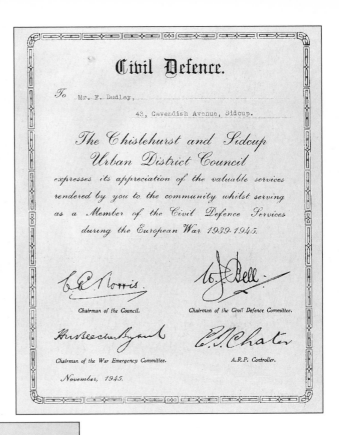

Civil Defence.

To Mr. F. Dudley,

43, Cavendish Avenue, Sidcup.

The Chislehurst and Sidcup Urban District Council expresses its appreciation of the valuable services rendered by you to the community whilst serving as a Member of the Civil Defence Services during the European War 1939-1945.

Chairman of the Council.

Chairman of the Civil Defence Committee.

Chairman of the War Emergency Committee.

A.R.P. Controller.

November, 1945.

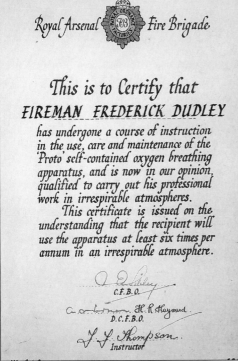

Royal Arsenal Fire Brigade

This is to Certify that

FIREMAN FREDERICK DUDLEY

has undergone a course of instruction in the use, care and maintenance of the 'Proto' self-contained oxygen breathing apparatus, and is now in our opinion, qualified to carry out his professional work in irrespirable atmospheres.

This certificate is issued on the understanding that the recipient will use the apparatus at least six times per annum in an irrespirable atmosphere.

C.F.B.O.

H. R. Hayward.
D.C.F.B.O.

J. J. Thompson.
Instructor

Frederick's certificate indicates the type of breathing apparatus he was qualified to use in fighting fires in 'irrespirable atmospheres'. Duty hours were eight hours on, eight hours off, driving a red Merryweather Fire Engine. 'It was hard driving in the black of night with no lights and tram lines along the way' he recalls.

The Fire Brigade moored their fire boats off Lambeth. These water cannon are capable of jetting to the top of high buildings on the river front or the top gallants of sailing ships and are also used in spectacular display during river pageants. PC John Bonnewell had a ringside view of this fireboat from his police launch in the 1980s.

Woolwich is part of the beat of Thames Division. Police regularly patrol the river from Teddington Lock to the Thames Estuary. Nearly all these wharves, pictured in 1974, have now disappeared.

Thames police on duty for the 1935 Jubilee of King George V: Buster Kitson, PC Storny, 'Rubber Face' Coleman, Bill Beckenburg, PC McConachy, Alex Hillian, George Henson and Bill Card, all in their naval referee-style jacket uniforms. MPTD.

To keep up with criminals operating on the river the police required speedier boats. A high speed, twin-screwed launch was developed, and Mr David Sherriff, Director of the FPA officially handed over the first to be completed to the Thames Division in the 1970s. The police flag lies ready to be put in position and unfurled for the maiden voyage. MPTD.

Cherry Garden Pier was popular with children: as well as enabling them to get to the water's edge, give or take the odd wall to climb over 'it was handy for a quick dip, provided the police were not watching from over at Wapping. If they saw us they'd come across in their launch and tell us off' said Sidney Fagan. MPTD.

Left: In 1940s the river was still polluted and the odd dead dog or cat floated by, but that did not stop children swimming there especially during the hot summer of 1947... Right: ... But the police knew what they were talking about when they warned of danger: More than one little lad was fished out of the water after it was too late to save him, and it was the sad duty of the police to inform his parents. MPTD.

In 1890 an ex-Royal Navy ship was used as a floating police station in the Thames for as long as it was seaworthy. The ship was then taken to Margate where it was beached. MPTD.

The Marine Police steam launch *Watch* with Inspector Garland, off Alexander's Pier, Wapping in 1900. Behind is a Sun tug. MPTD.

Ravensborough II, one of the Harbour Masters' launches patrolling during a barge rowing race to ensure the safety and compliance of regulations of both competitors and water-born spectators.

PC John Bonnewell and PC Frank Richards were on regular duty in their police launch near Tower Bridge. Thames division officers wear a distinctive, nautically-based uniform which includes an anchor tie-pin. In the early 1900s they still carried cutlasses rather than truncheons. Their duties are still to keep crime off the river.

Customs and Excise officers have to be alert to any crevices where goods can be smuggled. They are particularly on the look out for drugs, but it could also be diamonds, stolen paintings or spirits hidden behind an innocent-looking panel or guard on an incoming ship. HMC&E.

Customs Officers' uniforms in 1910 looked warmer than today's models, but then they worked in unheated, draughty halls, wharfside, and were expected to board ships under sail heading in from the sea in all weathers as well as mounting coastal patrols on horseback. HMC&E.

'The Smugglers Surprised by Revenue Men' reads the caption under this eighteenth century print. The Revenue Men, wearing sailor's uniform carry cutlasses, as did sailors of the day. The penalties for smuggling were draconian, so these men were literally fighting for their lives. HMC&E.

The Revenue Cutter, *Greyhound*, in pursuit of smugglers, early nineteenth century. Cutters were speedy ships carrying a lot of canvas for their size and weight and could usually out-manoeuvre the heavily-laden smugglers' boats, carrying illegal cargo to fullest capacity with gunwhales barely above water. HMC&E.

Eleven

Flotsam

'Flotsam and Jetsam' were an old music hall act. But in law jetsam is that which is deliberately thrown overboard, while flotsam is goods or other found floating, unattached, unassociated with anything in particular. This is a collection of things not easily catagorized.

Duke of *Albe-* as a Property justly acquired by them, as well by the
marle & al. Laws of Nations. as the *Civil Law.*
in Anno 1687.
17 E. 2. c. 11.   V. The *King* shall have Wreck of the Sea, Whales, and
great Sturgeons taken in the Sea, and elsewhere through-
out the whole Realm, except in Places privileged by
the *King.*

Sir *Henry Con-*   VI. By the Grant of Wreck will pass *Flotsam,* *Jetsam,*
stable's Case, and *Lagan,* when they are cast upon the Land ; but if
Coke 5 pars. they are not cast upon the Land, the Admiral hath Ju-
fol. 107. risdiction, and not the *Common Law,* and they cannot
be said Wreck.

5 Co. 106.   *Wreccum Maris,* are such Goods only as are cast and
5 Co. 106. b. left upon the Land by the Sea.

Flotsam, is when a Ship is sunk, or otherwise perished,
and the Goods float upon the Sea.

ibid.   *Jetsam,* is when the Ship is in danger to be sunk, and
for lightning the Ship, the Goods are cast into the Sea,
notwithstanding which the Ship perisheth.

ibid.   *Lagan vel Ligan,* is when the Goods being heavy, are
cast into the Sea before the Ship perishes, which by the
Prudence of the Master or Mariners, who have an In-
tent to save them so sunk, as that they may come at them
again ; in order to which they fasten a Buoy or other
light Matter, that may signifie to them where they lie,
if Providence should bring them in a Condition to retake
them.

46 E. 3. 15.   The King shall have *Flotsam,* *Jetsam* and *Lagan,* when
Auth. Omnes the Ship perisheth, or when the Owners of the Goods
perigrini com- are not known ; but when the Ship perishes not, *è con-*
munia de sue- tra.
cessibus acq.
per Leg. Oleron   A Man may have *Flotsam* and *Jetsam* by the King's
Grant ; and may have *Flotsam* within the high and low
Coke 5. part. Water-mark by Prescription, as it appears by those of
fol. 107. the West-Countries, who prescribe to have Wreck in
Coke 2 Instit. the Sea ; so far as they may see a *Humber* Barrel.
fol. 167.
Leg. 8. D. de   VII. If the Ship be ready to perish, and all the Men
lig. Rhod. de therein, for Safeguard of their Lives, leave the Ship,
and after the forsaken Ship perishes, if any of the Men
be saved and come to Land, the Goods are not lost.

A Ship on the Sea was pursued by Enemies, the Men
therein for Safeguard of their Lives, forsake the Ship,
the Enemies take the Ship, and spoils her of her Goods
and

and Tackle, and turn her to Sea ; by stress of Weather 5 R. 2. pro
she is cast on Land, where it happened her Men arrived : *Willielmo Fish-*
It was resolved by all the Judges of *England,* that the *f. 167. Leg.* *lake Co. 2 Inst.*
Ship was no Wreck, nor lost.   43. §. 11. D.
de furt.

VIII. If Goods are cast up as a Wreck, and it falls out Pl.Com. 466.
they be *bona petitura,* the Sheriff may sell them within
the Year, and the Sale is good ; but he must account to
the true Owners.

Owners claiming the Wreck, must make their Proof by F. N. B. fol.
their Marks or Cocquets, by the Book of Customs, or by 112. c. The
the Testimony of honest Men ; and if the Wreck belongs Year and Day
to the King, the Party may sue out a Commission to hear shall be ac-
and determine, and that by the Oaths of twelve Men ; or counted from
else he may bring his Action at Law, and make out his the Seizure,
Proof by *Verdict* ; but such Action must be brought *with-* 2 Inst. 168.
in the Year and Day.   5 Co. 107. b.

Note, Flotsam, Jetsam and *Lagan,* are Goods on or in 5 Co. 126. b.
the Sea, and belong to the King, who by Charter hath
granted them to the Lord Admiral.

IX. If Goods were wreckt on the Shore, and the Lord Left unresol-
having Power, takes them, he shall not pay Custom, nei- ved in *Mour*
fol. 224. But
since adjudg-
ed in C. B. upon a special Verdict found at St. *Edmund's Bury in Suffolk.*

ther by the *Common Law* nor by the Statute ; for at the Shep. versus
Common Law, wrecked Goods could not be charged with *Gosuold, Hill.*
Custom, because at the *Common Law* all *Wreck* was whol- 23, 24 Car. 2.
ly the Kings, and he could not have a small Duty of Cu- *Rot.* 615.
stom out of that which was all his own ; and by *Weston. 159.* *Vaughan, fol.*
1. where wrecked Goods belonged more to another than
to the King, he shall have it in like manner, that is, as
the King hath his.

Now Goods that are chargeable with Custom, according to the Act of *Tunnage and Poundage,* must have these
Properties.

1. They must be Goods which shall come or be brought 12 Car. 2. c 4.
into the Ports or Places of the Kingdom.

2. They must come or be brought into such *Ports* or
Places, as *Merchandize* that is for sale, and to that end ;
for there can be no other Conception of *Goods* brought
as *Merchandize.*

    3. They

The laws and usage of flotsam, jetsam, shipwrecked goods and overweight cargo according to Charles Molloy in his *Treatise of Affairs Maritime and of Commerce,* 'Printed for John Walthos junior, over-against the Royal Exchange in Cornhill and J. Wotton at the Three Daggers in Fleet Street, 1722.'

4. Movement in Docks—Not Entering River.

Charges for services as Waterman acting as Helmsman or Dock Pilot, on board vessels, together with boat service, shifting from berth to berth, berth to Dry Dock or vice versa, in any one Group of Docks not necessitating the vessel entering the River.

Vessels.		Total Cost.	The total cost is apportioned as under.	
			These charges will only be paid if services are rendered.	
			Dock Pilot.	Boat & 2 men unmooring & remooring.
Gross Tons	Gross Tons	£ s. d.	£ s. d.	£ s. d.
Up to 1,000		3 14 6	1 19 0	1 15 6
Over 1,000 up to 2,000		4 3 0	2 4 0	1 19 0
,, 2,000 ,, 4,000		5 5 0	2 16 6	2 8 6
,, 4,000 ,, 6,000		5 15 0	3 3 0	2 12 0
,, 6,000 ,, 10,000		6 4 0	3 9 0	2 15 0
,, 10,000 ,, 15,000		7 1 0	4 2 6	2 18 6
,, 15,000 ,, 20,000		7 17 6	4 16 0	3 1 6
,, 20,000		8 9 0	5 4 6	3 4 6

The above applies to vessels temporarily shifting or hauling off and includes unmooring and remooring.

Extra Quaymen when engaged for shifting from berth to berth (**excluding movement to and from Dry Dock**) to be paid 22/6 per man instead of 18/- per man as set out in Scale 11 as compensation for the extra work involved.

When the mooring and remooring operation with a boat and 2 men is carried out without a Waterman on board, the charges will be as set out in the last column above.

As for Watermen and Lightermen on general river work, dock and river pilots had their own scale of charges as scheduled by the PLA and agreed between the Shipping Federation Ltd, the Thames District Committee and the Tugmen's Guild on 14 February, 1955. The Tugman's Guild Secretary was A.T. Kirk.

5. Movement in Docks—Entering River.

Charges for services rendered as Waterman, acting as Helmsman or Dock Pilot (not including River Pilotage) transporting vessel from berth in Dock (including Dry Dock) in any one group of Docks, to berth (including Dry Dock) in any other group of Docks, necessitating the vessel entering the River. The charges to include Boat and two men at each group of Docks and in the River, unmooring and remooring at berth or Dry Dock as the case may be.

VESSELS.		Total Cost.	The total cost is apportioned as under.					
			These charges will only be paid if services are rendered.					
			First Dock.		River.		Second Dock.	
			Dock Pilot.	Boat & 2 men unmooring.	Helmsman.	Boat and 2 men for headrope.	Dock Pilot.	Boat & 2 men mooring.
Gross Tons	Gross Tons	£ s. d.	£ s. d.	£ s. d.	£ s. d.	£ s. d.	£ s. d.	£ s. d.
Up to 1,000		8 8 6	1 16 6	1 8 6	1 5 6	13 0	1 16 6	1 8 6
Over 1,000 up to 2,000		9 3 0	2 0 0	1 10 6	1 7 6	14 6	2 0 0	1 10 6
,, 2,000 ,, 4,000		11 15 0	2 15 0	1 16 0	1 15 6	17 6	2 15 0	1 16 0
,, 4,000 ,, 6,000		12 12 6	3 0 0	1 16 0	2 1 6	19 0	3 0 0	1 16 0
,, 6,000 ,, 10,000		14 5 6	3 8 6	1 19 0	2 7 6	1 3 0	3 8 6	1 19 0
,, 10,000 ,, 15,000		16 17 6	4 2 6	2 3 0	3 1 0	1 5 6	4 2 6	2 3 0
,, 15,000 ,, 20,000		19 9 0	5 0 0	2 5 6	3 10 0	1 8 0	5 0 0	2 5 6
,, 20,000		20 15 0	5 13 0	2 5 6	3 10 0	1 8 0	5 13 0	2 5 6

In 1970-1980 when train strikes dogged the lives of commuters an attempt was made to establish a river service to the City with seven river buses run by Thamesline. Robert Crouch was Managing Director. Olympia and York bought the company when building Canary Wharf, enlarging the service with several catamarans. Landing points were established along both riverbanks between Greenwich and Westminster. Lack of funding ended the service in 1993. Now only three vessels remain, unused, bobbing at anchor in St. Katherine's Dock: the rest were purchased by a Far East operation which later sold one boat for the price they had paid for them all.

Poplar, Blackwall and District Rowing Club

President : W. J. Woodward Fisher Esq.

Headquarters—"Princess of Wales" Barque St. E.14 (P. Muggleton)

present Race for the

PUBLICAN'S FOURS

AND INVITATION SCULLING RACE

Sunday, 25th October, 1959

Starter and Umpire—
GEORGE EDWARD COLE Snr.

Distance Judges—
J. WISEMAN & C. GODDEN

Boat Stewards—
R. McPHERSON, J. ORWELL, L. GOUDIE, E. LELK

Course for all Races
Millwall Docks to the Island Gardens

PROGRAMME 3d.

Greenwich Regatta, revived after the war, was held every August Bank Holiday Monday (then at the beginning of the month) with seventeen events, including a Ladies Fours and Ladies sculls races. The gala ran from 10.00 to 16.30hrs. The Subscribers' Enclosure was provided by the Royal Naval College. Len Coker's team won the Novice Fours.

One of the less pleasant duties of a Thames police officer is retrieving the bodies of the drowned. In the old carpenter's workshop, now a museum, is an early grappling hook used for dredging corpses from the river bed. As can be imagined this was rather rough on the corpse and modern, efficient methods are now used says PC Gotch; the duties are mainly carried out by frogmen.

Tidal rivers have a tendency to silt up as mud, gravel and debris shift with the ebb and flow. As sea-going vessels navigate the Thames it is important to ensure a sufficiently clear channel to take these deeper-drafted ships. In the early 1900s twin-bucketed steam dredgers operated regularly, ploughing along the river bed and scooping out a channel as it went. The residue was dumped at sea. PLA

The Association of Master Lightermen and Barge Owners.

Telephone : MANsion House 1415-6-7-8 & 9111-2.
Secretary : E. J. G. WEARE.

PLANTATION HOUSE,
FENCHURCH STREET,
LONDON E.C.3

The following are the adjusted rates of pay for men engaged in the Lighterage Industry to operate on and from 6 a.m. **Monday, 20th May, 1957.** These rates are shown as including all differentials.

QUAY LIGHTERMEN, WATCHMEN AND APPRENTICES.

MONDAY 6 a.m. to SATURDAY 5 p.m.

DAY'S PAY :

		s.	d.
Lightermen and Watchmen		37	0
Apprentices, First six months		12	7
Second six months		16	0
2nd year		22	10
3rd year		28	11

OVERTIME, 6 a.m. to 8 a.m. and 5 p.m. to 8 p.m. (and Saturday afternoon) :

Lightermen and Watchmen	per hour	6	2
Apprentices, First six months	,, ,,	2	1
Second six months	,, ,,	2	8
2nd year	,, ,,	3	10
3rd year	,, ,,	4	10

NIGHT WORK, 8 p.m. TO MIDNIGHT (MINIMUM PAYMENT 3 HOURS) :

Lightermen and Watchmen	per hour	6	11
Apprentices, First six months	,, ,,	2	4
Second six months	,, ,,	3	0
2nd year	,, ,,	4	3
3rd year	,, ,,	5	5

NIGHT WORK, 8 p.m. to 6 a.m. (10 HOURS AT NIGHT-WORK RATE) :

Lightermen and Watchmen	total payment	69	2
Apprentices, First six months	,, ,,	—	
Second six months	,, ,,	—	
2nd year	,, ,,	42	6
3rd year	,, ,,	54	2

WORKING ON AFTER 6 a.m. TO COMPLETE A NIGHT'S JOB.

LIGHTERMEN AND WATCHMEN :

(a) started 6 a.m. previous day : per hour after 6 a.m.	...	9	3
(b) started 7 a.m. previous day : ,, ,, to 7 a.m.	...	6	11
,, ,, ,, ,, ,, ,, after 7 a.m.	...	9	3
(c) started 8 a.m. previous day : ,, ,, to 8 a.m.	...	6	11
,, ,, ,, ,, ,, ,, after 8 a.m.	...	9	3

APPRENTICES—2nd year :

(a) started 6 a.m. previous day : per hour after 6 a.m.	...	5	9
(b) started 7 a.m. previous day : ,, ,, to 7 a.m.	...	4	3
,, ,, ,, ,, ,, ,, after 7 a.m.	...	5	9
(c) started 8 a.m. previous day : ,, ,, to 8 a.m.	...	4	3
,, ,, ,, ,, ,, ,, after 8 a.m.	...	5	9

APPRENTICES—3rd year :

(a) started 6 a.m. previous day : per hour after 6 a.m.	...	7	3
(b) started 7 a.m. previous day : ,, ,, to 7 a.m.	...	5	5
,, ,, ,, ,, ,, ,, after 7 a.m.	...	7	3
(c) started 8 a.m. previous day : ,, ,, to 8 a.m.	...	5	5
,, ,, ,, ,, ,, ,, after 8 a.m.	...	7	3

SATURDAY 5 p.m. to MONDAY 6 a.m.

OVERTIME, 5 p.m. to 8 p.m. SATURDAY AND 6 a.m. to 8 a.m. and 5 p.m. to 8 p.m. SUNDAY :

		s.	d.
Lightermen and Watchmen	per hour	8	8
Apprentices, First six months	,, ,,	3	5
Second six months	,, ,,	4	2
2nd year	,, ,,	4	9
3rd year	,, ,,	6	7

Watermen, Lightermen and Apprentices' pay was strictly regulated to ensure uniformity, otherwise some firms would pay less than the minimum, while larger firms able to offer higher wages would push smaller concerns out of business.

Greenfield Sports formed a highly successful Stevedores and Dockers Football Team. They were winners yet again in 1947. Len Coker is second from the left, second row from the back.

The hand on the ship's telegraph is that of tug skipper Maurice Jones aboard *Plantina*.

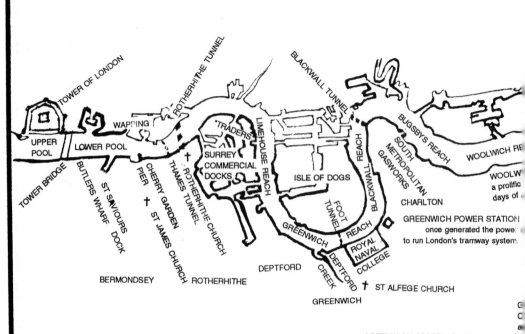

N

NOT TO SCALE

TOWER OF LONDON

ROTHERHITHE TUNNEL

BLACKWALL TUNNEL

WAPPING

UPPER POOL

LOWER POOL

TOWER BRIDGE

BUTLERS WHARF DOCK

ST SAVIOURS DOCK

CHERRY GARDEN PIER

THAMES TUNNEL

ROTHERHITHE CHURCH

ST JAMES CHURCH

TRADERS

SURREY COMMERCIAL DOCKS

LIMEHOUSE REACH

ISLE OF DOGS

FOOT TUNNEL

GREENWICH REACH

BLACKWALL REACH

SOUTH METROPOLITAN GASWORKS

BUGSBYS REACH

WOOLWICH RE

WOOLW

a prolific

days of

CHARLTON

GREENWICH POWER STATION
once generated the power
to run London's tramway system.

DEPTFORD

DEPTFORD CREEK

ROYAL NAVAL COLLEGE

ST ALFEGE CHURCH

GREENWICH

BERMONDSEY

ROTHERHITHE

GREENWICH OBSERVATORY
was built in 1675 by Charles II for
his Royal Observor, Flamstead, and is
known for being the position of O° from
which all longitude is measured.

BERMONDSEY once boasted
a Benedictine Abbey. Sir John
Falstaff, renowned in "The Merry
Wives of Windsor" is reputed to
have owned a house here. There
were many pleasure gardens here,
preserved in such names as Cherry
Gardens, Spa Road etc. Wharves
once stretched along the whole
riverbank and Bermondsey was
famous for its tanneries. It is part
of The Pool of London (from
London Bridge to Limehouse).

ROTHERHITHE:
During the reign of Edward III
a great fleet was prepared here
for Edward, the Black Prince
to invade France.
Whalers once set forth from
Greenland Dock, the first of the
Surrey Commercial Docks opened
in 1809 and developed over the
19th century.

THE THAMES TUNNEL runs between
Rotherhithe and Wapping. Designed by
Brunel, it was completed in 1843 after
taking twenty years to build and was
regarded as an emgineering marvel. It was
the forerunner of the modern Underground
railway system and is still in use.

DEPTFORD and DEPTFORD CREEK:
The north-east boundary between Surrey
and Kent is the Ravensbourne stream
which becomes Deptford Creek as it reaches
the Thames. Deptford centred around the
Royal Naval victualling yard and Reserve
Supply Depot, located on the south shore
between Limehouse and Greenwich Reaches.
It was formerly known as the Royal Dockyard,
founded by Queen Elizabeth I and was
renowned for its shipbuilding.

126

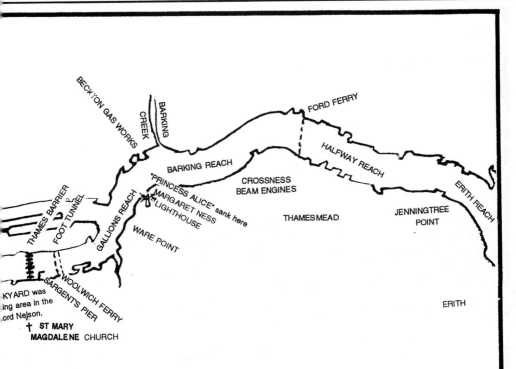

BECKTON GAS WORKS

BARKING CREEK

FORD FERRY

HALFWAY REACH

BARKING REACH

CROSSNESS
BEAM ENGINES

"PRINCESS ALICE" sank here

MARGARET NESS
LIGHTHOUSE

THAMESMEAD

ERITH REACH

JENNINGTREE
POINT

THAMES BARRIER

FOOT TUNNEL

GALLIONS REACH

WARE POINT

WOOLWICH FERRY

SARGENT'S PIER

ERITH

KYARD was
...ing area in the
...ord Nelson.

† ST MARY
MAGDALENE CHURCH

WOOLWICH FERRY offers free
transportation across the river from
South to North Woolwich and back
for all road vehicles and pedestrians.

...CH ROYAL NAVAL
...was built on the site of
...ace and was mainly designed
...istopher Wren for Queen
...o wished to provide a
...home and hospital for
...n. It was later converted for
...Royal Naval College and
...aritime Museum.

ROYAL ARSENAL, WOOLWICH:
This site was built as a weapons manufacturing
and storage area by Henry VIII and was in
continuous use as such until the 1980s.
Until recently the area was out of bounds
to the general public. The old Mulberry
wharves used to load tanks aboard ships
during World War I can still be seen.

ERITH was well-known for
its moulding sand which was
of high quality and generated
orders from overseas.

CHURCH SPIRES were an important part of the riverscape .
They were used as landmarks by ships finding their way up the
Thames to their berth. Now, these guiding spires are largely
overshadowed by modern high-rise buildings.

TOWER BRIDGE to THAMESMEAD

HH

Epilogue

For over 2,000 years, the River Thames has provided the area of London with a natural, self-maintaining highway. However, when the Romans built the first City, it was created near enough to the sea for it to become an international port. For hundreds of years, the port's cargo activities were pre-eminent and depressed the use of the River Thames through London for passenger transport.

Some twenty-five–thirty years ago, with the advent of modern cargo handling methods such as containerisation, ro-ro ships, etc., the port cargo work was transferred down-River to Tilbury as using the London Docks proved to be too time-consuming and expensive. This left our natural highway as an option once more for passenger transport use, as well as for leisure and pleasure.

Several attempts have been made by private companies to provide Londoners with a River transport service. None of these have been given adequate backing by the Governments of the day (of any persuasion) who, whilst seeing sense in paying £2,000,000 for one mile of motorway, did not seem able to accept that this same amount could provide an integral East-West route through London using the River highway. This amount, unlike the motorway costs, would also include provision of the vessels required for such a service.

We trust and hope that a properly appraised plan for the use of the wonderful natural benefit offered by the River Thames, will eventually come to fruition.

Robert George Crouch
Bargemaster to H.M. the Queen
Clerk to The Company of Watermen and Lightermen
16 St Mary-at-Hill, London

The *Royal Nore*: the Royal Barge is only decked out with her impressive accoutrements, including the Royal Standard, when in a State Water Procession or when carrying a member of the Royal Family. Otherwise she travels 'in mufti', with Standard, silver dolphins and other embellishments removed. When HM the Queen is aboard the full complement of eight Royal Bargemen are in attendance, with six for Prince Charles and four for lesser Royals. Capable of 22 knots the *Nore* normally travels at a more sedate 8-9 knots.